HEARTS OF GOLD

Reflections of

ADVOCACY

Gold Award Girl Scouts

Sheryl M Robinson

Copyright Page

Published by Grow and Share Network, LLC
First Edition, 2026

ISBN: 978-1-972135-05-1

Printed in the United States of America

Books in the Hearts of Gold Series

- *Earth Guardian*
- *STEM*
- *Creative Voice*
- *Health*
- *Inclusion*
- *Advocacy*
- *Community Connector*

Table of Contents

Chapter 1
What Advocacy Looks Like

The Spark Of Service

Advocacy often begins in the quietest moments of observation, when a young person notices a gap between how the world is and how it should be. One story in this book follows a girl who volunteers at a wildlife refuge, where the natural music of dragonflies is interrupted by the harsh roar of a highway. She watched as turtles and deer met tragic ends just feet from safety, and she realized these animals didn't have a voice to ask drivers to slow down. Her background as an animal lover turned a sad sight into a call to action, leading her to dream of a campaign that would bridge the gap between human progress and the natural world. She didn't want just to be a witness to a problem; she wanted to be the solution. This pattern of moving from a witness to a leader is a common thread among the advocates you will meet.

Another narrative began in the corners of a local community center, where a teenager noticed older students intimidating younger ones. This scene struck a chord because it mirrored her own history; she had been both the one picked on and the one being mean. Realizing how her actions affected others, she made a conscious effort to change her character and decided that no other child should feel that isolation. She recognized that younger kids often look up to high schoolers more than adults, and she decided to harness that "cool factor" to create a ripple effect of kindness. Her challenge was to build a bridge from the ground up, connecting students across generations to foster empathy. By standing in the gap, she proved that one person could hold a community together. These stories show that growth often comes from turning a personal realization into a structured plan. Whether it is protecting silent creatures or building a foundation for social change, the impact begins when a girl decides that her voice has the power to change the social fabric of her world.

Modern Bridges Of Innovation

In a rapidly changing world, advocacy also means ensuring that no one is left behind in the civic deserts or the bright traps of modern technology. One advocate in these pages grew up in a library, seeing it as the heartbeat of her town. However, she noticed her peers were disconnected from local life, sitting on the sidelines because they lacked the motivation to participate. She realized that even in thriving towns, teens can live in a civic drought. Her action was to build a bridge to belonging, using her discipline as a competitive athlete and public speaker to coordinate with government officials and librarians. She proved that participating in town life shouldn't have to wait until adulthood and that a girl with a plan can turn a desert into a thriving community garden.

Similarly, another story explores engineering as a tool for inclusion. A robotics team captain realized that not every child had access to the STEM opportunities she enjoyed. She saw a gap in outreach at a local center, where portable activities were lacking to engage children on the streets. Her mission was to turn scrap wood into a mobile classroom, showing younger students they could be engineers too. She used a formal engineering design process to create a design loop in which failure was an opportunity to improve. Her growth was found in the numbers—reaching 300 students a semester—and in her own transition from a shy student to a leader who engineers a life filled with success.

The digital world presents its own set of challenges, where access to media often moves faster than the instructions on how to use it safely. One leader observed the bright trap of the screen, where catchy thumbnails lure kids into unsafe content. She decided to provide a safety net through media literacy, teaching peers to navigate the colorful mazes of social media with wisdom. She had to be positive even when her early sessions were empty, eventually reaching a global audience and influencing state-level educational change. These advocates show that whether through a wooden racetrack, a civic workshop, or a digital compass, a girl's voice can influence how a community—and even a state—educates its children.

Voices For Policy And Equity

True leadership often requires stepping into professional spaces where youth voices are rarely heard, from school boardrooms to the halls of state legislatures. One advocate in this book, navigating the world through a neurodiversity lens, realized that her teachers were relying on outdated information. She founded an affinity group to provide a safe harbor and eventually took on the mission of educating the educators. She challenged the ten-year cycle of teacher training, insisting that students with unique needs couldn't wait a decade for their teachers to catch up. Her persistence changed her school's policy and sparked her entrepreneurial spirit, leading her to join national advisory boards. She widened the threshold of the schoolhouse so every mind could flourish.

Other stories highlight the bare necessities of kindness and the shield of public health. One girl expanded a simple sock drive into a monumental mission, reaching eight schools and ensuring that no student had to worry about basic dignity while learning. She managed a sorting room army and learned that leadership is about finding the gaps and being brave enough to fill them. Meanwhile, another teen pivoted during a global pandemic to address the fear of medical procedures. She created distraction kits for vaccination sites, turning a moment of panic for a child into a memory of success. She proved that looking out for the smallest members of a community makes the entire world stronger.

Finally, you will read about those who took their seat at the national table. One thirteen-year-old entered the fast-paced world of political campaigns, often being the youngest person in the room. She turned her personal struggles with being unheard into a program that empowered her entire generation to make them listen. Another visionary looked at the digital frontier and prepared to influence state laws. They noticed a gap in protections for children in family vlogs and worked with legal experts to draft legislation. They proved that a single person's vision can influence the laws that govern millions. Together, these themes of

environment, safety, equity, and policy form a
tapestry of what advocacy looks like today.

Chapter 2
Engineering Imagination

Emma Kessner (Ep 12)

The Spark of Tinkering

For Emma Kessner, the city of Los Angeles was a giant laboratory waiting to be explored. Growing up with a father who worked as a math and computer science instructor, science and technology weren't just subjects in a textbook; they were dinner-table conversations that fueled her curiosity. Emma spent much of her childhood looking for ways to combine her love for making things with her desire to understand how the world functioned. This passion led her to become a captain of an all-girls robotics team, where she learned that engineering was as much about creativity as it was about complex calculations. However, she knew that not every child in her community had the same access to the STEM opportunities she had enjoyed. She wanted to take the excitement of the robotics lab and bring it to students who might not even know what the word engineering meant.

Her search for a meaningful mission led her to a unique organization called the Rediscover Center. The center was a wonderland for anyone who loved to build, encouraging imagination and tinkerers to create with reused materials. It was a place where old wood, scrap metal, and discarded plastics transformed into works of art or functional machines. When Emma met with the center's leaders, she discovered a significant gap in their outreach. While they had incredible activities for children who visited their main location for summer and winter camps, they struggled when they volunteered at local schools or farmers' markets. They lacked high-quality, easily transportable activities to engage children in the streets and classrooms of Los Angeles.

Emma saw an opportunity to use her robotics background to solve this problem. She realized that if she could design a portable, engaging activity that taught children the basics of engineering, she could help the Rediscover Center significantly expand its reach. She decided that her project would focus on building a portable racetrack and a corresponding curriculum. Her goal was to show younger students that they could be engineers too, using simple materials to design, test, and improve their own race cars. She believed that if children became enthusiastic about science at a young age, they would be much more likely to pursue those interests later in life. With a plan in mind and a passion for tinkering, Emma set out to turn a pile of scrap wood into a mobile classroom of innovation.

The Art of the Pitch

Even with a strong background in robotics, Emma soon realized that the most difficult part of her project wasn't the building—it was the paperwork and professional communication required to get a project off the ground. She found the proposal process to be a steep learning curve. To succeed, a girl must do more than just have a good idea; she must learn to pitch that idea to an organization, write professional emails, and follow up when people are busy. Emma was lucky to attend a school that taught her how to address teachers and professionals properly, but she noticed many of her peers struggled with these skills. She recognized that the ability to write a clear, concise email or deliver a thirty-second pitch was the primary thing that separated the girls who finished their projects from those who didn't.

Emma had to treat her project like a professional business venture. She spent weeks refining her proposal, ensuring it didn't just sound like a fun afternoon activity but a sustainable program with a lasting impact on the community. She had to learn the importance of persistence. When she didn't hear back from a contact immediately, she didn't take it personally. Instead, she learned to send polite follow-up messages to keep her project moving forward. This professional development experience was just as valuable as the technical work she was doing. She was learning that leadership required a high level of organization and the confidence to speak up for her vision, even when she felt like an introvert who would rather be working quietly on a robot.

To prepare for the challenges ahead, Emma participated in a project boot camp organized by her local council. These sessions gave her a head start on the smaller details of the process that she hadn't considered. She learned how to find the right project advisor and how to navigate the interview process with the council committee. This support network was crucial for Emma, as it enabled her to turn her spark of an idea into a robust plan that met the rigorous standards for a top-level project. By the time her proposal was approved, Emma had already grown significantly as a communicator. She was no longer just a student with a dream; she was a project manager with an action plan and the professional skills to see it through to the end.

From Scrap Wood to Speed

Once the proposal received approval, the real tinkering began. Emma decided to fully embrace the Rediscover Center's philosophy by building her portable racetrack entirely from reused materials, adding a layer of complexity to her engineering process. She couldn't just order perfect parts from a catalog; she had to look at piles of donated wood and determine which pieces could be sanded and repurposed for her track. She used her experience from her robotics team to implement a formal engineering design process. She didn't want to build just a track that looked good; it was about creating a system that would enable students to learn to edit and revisit their original plans based on how their cars performed.

Emma's workshop became a hub of sawdust and prototypes. She spent hours testing different angles for the track and ensuring that the materials she used would be durable enough to survive being moved from school to school. To keep her project organized and ensure that every step contributed to a successful outcome, she followed a very specific development cycle:

Designing using cardboard and small scraps to find the most effective slope for the race cars.

Testing the track with students at the Rediscover Center to gather feedback on which parts of the race were the most exciting and which were too difficult.

Building the final version of the track using high-quality reused wood that was sanded and sealed to withstand heavy use at outdoor events.

Creating a detailed curriculum that walked teachers through the engineering design process, ensuring they could lead the activity without Emma being present.

The result of this hard work was a sleek, portable, easy-to-set-up system. But Emma knew that the track was only half of the solution. She also had to write a curriculum that was easy for children to understand. She wanted the kids to feel like they were part of a design loop. If their car fell off the track, she didn't want them to feel like they'd failed; she wanted them to ask why it fell off and how they could adjust the wheels or the car's weight to keep it on the track next time. This focus on improving the car each time was the heart of her educational mission. By the time she delivered the finished track to the center, she had created a resource that didn't just provide a toy, but a way for hundreds of students to think like engineers for the very first time.

Five Miles and a Heavy Banner

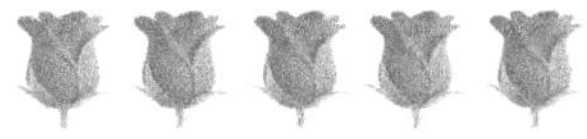

Sometimes Gold Award projects lead to unplanned outcomes. The confidence Emma built during her project led to an opportunity she never expected: the chance to walk in the Rose Parade in Pasadena. In Los Angeles, Gold Award Girl Scouts are invited to interview for a spot in the Tournament Troop. It was a scary process, but Emma's experience with public speaking and pitching her project had prepared her for success. She was selected as one of the fifty girls to walk in the New Year's Day parade, but soon discovered that the honor came with a grueling training schedule. It wasn't enough to just show up in a uniform; she had to spend her weekends at a local high school track, walking for five miles at a time while holding a heavy metal pole.

The training was surprisingly physical and tiring. Holding a banner pole in the exact right position for hours is not a natural movement, and Emma's arms would often ache after a practice session. To prepare at home, the troop leaders told the girls to practice walking around their neighborhoods while holding soda cans to build arm strength. Emma would walk through her LA neighborhood, focusing on her posture and her pace, preparing for the five-and-a-half-mile route of the parade. The discipline required for this was a perfect reflection of the discipline she had applied to her engineering project. She was learning that some of the most rewarding experiences in life require a massive amount of effort behind the scenes that no one ever sees.

The day of the parade was a whirlwind of sensory experiences. Emma had to be at the meeting house at 3:00 a.m., long before the sun rose over the California hills. It was cold as the girls got dressed in their uniforms, and they had to have their jackets taken away hours before the parade started to ensure they were ready for the news trucks and cameras. Emma participated in a flag-raising ceremony and then began the long walk past the award-winning floats. Seeing the Rose Court and the massive, flower-covered floats up close was an experience she would never forget. Walking that route, she realized how far she had come from the shy girl who first walked into the Rediscover Center. She was now a confident representative of her community, literally carrying a banner of achievement through the streets of her city.

Inclusive Innovation

Emma's project's success was found in the numbers and the smiles of the students who used her track. By the time her final report was submitted, her portable racetrack and curriculum were being used by as many as 300 elementary and middle school students every semester across 11 schools. The Rediscover Center had a high-quality activity they could take to farmers' markets and community fairs, fulfilling Emma's dream of making STEM inclusive for everyone. She had transformed a local problem into a sustainable solution that would continue to inspire young tinkers for years after she graduated.

The growth Emma experienced during her project didn't stop with the racetrack. Inspired by the business and leadership skills she gained, she co-founded a student apprenticeship program at her high school. After the school library was renovated and a new cafe was installed, Emma noticed it was only open during limited hours. She wanted to allow students to buy food whenever they wanted while also learning business skills. She helped organize a club where students ran the cafe, managed inventory, handled a cash register, and even negotiated with vendors to find products they could sell for a profit. The club was so successful that soon talk began of turning it into an official class. Emma had proven that she could identify a need and build a team to solve it, whether it involved scrap wood or a high school coffee shop.

Looking toward her future, Emma has set her sights on becoming an astrophysicist or an astronomical engineer. She wants to continue pushing herself into male-dominated fields and show other girls that they belong in the highest levels of science. She also wants to remain a well-rounded person, balancing her love for technology with her passion for reading, writing, and art. She credits her project for giving her the self-confidence to put herself out there and speak in front of large crowds. She encourages every young girl to tackle their own projects, telling them that the journey of self-discovery is worth every hour of work.

Emma Kessner discovered that engineering isn't just about building things; it's about building a better way for people to see themselves. Her portable track was more than a wooden frame for toy cars; it was a physical bridge that carried the light of science into the corners of her community that needed it most. Emma spent years warming up to her own potential, proving that when you dare to tinker with your own limits, you can engineer a life that is both structurally sound and filled with sweetness. She is a reminder that the most durable things we build are not made of wood or metal, but of the confidence we gain when we decide to follow our passion into the light of success.

Chapter 3
Guarding the Digital Gateway

Lakshanya Rajaganapathi (Ep 114)

Bright Trap Of The Screen

Lakshanya Rajaganapathi, known to her friends as Lana, was a teenager who spent much of her time looking at the world through a digital lens. Like most people her age, she navigated the colorful mazes of Snapchat and the curated squares of Instagram daily. However, while others were simply scrolling, Lana was observing. She started noticing a troubling pattern in the news and among her peers. People were struggling. They were getting caught in the web of catfishing, falling for misinformation, and feeling the heavy weight of social media's negative side. It occurred to her that access to media is often allowed at a rate much faster than the rate of literacy instruction. We are given the tools to connect before we are given the manual on how to protect ourselves. This realization became the spark for her mission.

She wanted to protect the next generation from the pitfalls she saw every day. To make her point clear to younger children, Lana developed a clever analogy. She remembered being a little girl in the supermarket, tugging on her mother's sleeve and pointing at a box on a shelf. She didn't want the cereal because of the ingredients; she wanted it because the packaging was bright, neon, and exciting. She asked the elementary students she worked with if they had ever felt that same pull toward a colorful box, and almost every hand in the room shot up. Lana then connected this to the digital world. She explained that YouTube thumbnails are exactly like that cereal box. They use bright colors and exciting pictures to get you to click, but just like a sugary cereal might not be good for your body, the content behind that bright thumbnail might not be safe for your mind.

Lana's motivation was deeply rooted in a desire to provide tips and tricks for navigating the internet safely. She didn't want to give a boring lecture that sounded like an adult telling kids what to do. She knew that children often tune out adults, so she designed her project to feel like a talk from a peer. Her goal was to create a dialogue where students could ask questions and reflect on their own habits. She wanted to bridge the gap between having an iPad in your hand and having the wisdom to use it correctly. This media literacy project was her way of ensuring that the digital world remained a place of connection rather than danger.

Silence Of A Saturday Morning

When Lana began organizing her media literacy sessions at the local library, she expected the community to jump at the opportunity. She had her curriculum ready and her analogies polished. However, she quickly encountered a major hurdle that many leaders face: getting people to show up. Her first few sessions were quiet—painfully quiet. On a Saturday morning, most kids would rather sleep in or play outside than sit in a library learning about the internet. Lana admitted that at one point, the low turnout was so discouraging that she turned to her mother and asked, "Can we just not do these sessions anymore? Nobody is showing up."

Lana had a choice: to let the project fade away or to find a way to pivot and persist. She realized that she needed to think like a marketer. She went to the library staff she was working with and asked for advice on how to grab people's attention. She decided to change her approach by physically going into the children's room at the library and speaking directly to the parents. She started offering small incentives, like candy and chocolate, to get the kids engaged and loosen them up. She learned that a leader must be insistent on their goals, even when the initial response is cold.

Her persistence paid off. By the second session, the room transformed from having only three people to being filled with nearly twenty students. Once the kids were in the room, Lana made sure it didn't feel like a classroom. She turned it into a Q&A, where students jumped out of their seats, eager to raise their hands. One fourth grader asked a question that truly shocked Lana: "How can Instagram and Snapchat be so bad?" It was in that moment that Lana realized just how much her work was needed. These kids only saw the "cool" side of being online. They didn't see how a single word or a single post could flip someone's world upside down. By overcoming her own discouragement, Lana was able to provide these students with a safety net they didn't even know they were missing.

Global Blueprint For Safety

Lana's vision for her project extended beyond her own backyard. She understood that technology connects everyone around the world, meaning the dangers are universal. To create a project with significant global impact, she decided to take her curriculum to India. She worked with her grandfather and her aunt, who owned a school there, to organize a special session for the students during their school day. This international component required extensive coordination and a deep dive into the logistics of communication across different cultures and languages.

Lana focused on building a team and creating physical resources that would endure, ensuring the project executed perfectly. She had to learn how to delegate tasks and trust her team members to help her reach her goals. In India, she even recruited her cousins to help her prepare materials for the students. Her strategy for carrying out the mission included several vital steps:

Researching the core principles of media literacy to develop a 5-step navigation guide: Identify, Analyze, Evaluate, Create, and Act.

Translating all educational posters and handouts into the local language in India to ensure every student could read and understand the safety steps.

Collaborating with her grandfather to obtain donations of candy and custom-made pens printed with the message, "Be Mindful of Media Literacy."

Building a dedicated website that serves as a permanent hub where students can reflect on situations, watch instructional videos, and receive ongoing advice.

While in the classroom in India, Lana used another effective analogy to overcome the cultural gap. She held up a packet of chips that came with a small toy inside. She pointed out that kids often only buy the chips because they want the toy, but once they open the bag, they realize the chips aren't that good, and the toy isn't very fun either. She compared this to an internet "clickbait" rabbit hole. The students in India were just as engaged as those in America, and Lana was amazed to hear they were playing the same games, like Clash of Clans. This experience proved to her that her project wasn't just helping her city; it was helping the nation and the world. She had created a blueprint for a solution that could be used anywhere there was a screen and a student.

Creating A School Council

The measurable impact of Lana's project continued to grow as she brought her mission back to her own high school and the local middle school. She realized the way the schools were currently teaching media literacy wasn't very effective. Most teachers would simply hand out iPads and say, "Don't go on bad websites," knowing that the school administration was watching. Lana knew that this kind of top-down warning didn't teach students how to make good choices when no one was looking. She wanted to implement a system that would encourage students to help their peers.

She approached her local technology administrator with an ambitious idea: creating a Media Literacy Council. She was nervous about talking to a school administrator on such a high level, but she was thrilled when they were immediately on board. The council would have student representatives from each grade in the middle school. These representatives would be elected by their peers, fostering a sense of ownership and responsibility. Lana planned to meet with these representatives, give them tips and tricks on digital safety, and then have them return to their homerooms to share those ideas with the rest of the student body.

Creating the council wasn't just a one-time presentation; it was a permanent shift in the school's culture.

The success of her project even reached the ears of a state representative who attended one of her sessions. He was so impressed by her work that he suggested she send her project details to the Delaware Department of Education to use across the entire state system. Lana felt an incredible sense of pride knowing that her hard work would reach so many people. She had successfully transitioned from a girl with an idea into an advocate for state-level change. By the time her project was finalized, she had reached over a hundred people through her workshops and countless more through her digital presence. She moved the needle from simple internet use to intentional internet safety, proving that a girl's voice can indeed influence how a state educates its children.

Cookies To The Future

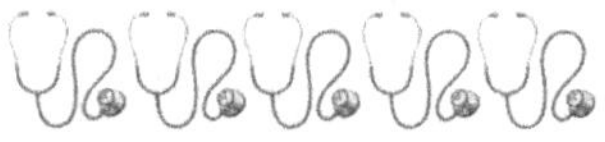

Reflecting on her journey, Lana realized that the project had changed her just as much as it had changed her community. She admitted that before she started, she was very shy and reserved. She had spent years in Girl Scouts, and she credited the simple act of selling cookies with helping her get out of her own shell. She remembered the courage it took, as a younger girl, to ask friends and family to support her cookie business, and she saw how those early steps laid the foundation for the leadership she displayed during her project. She was now doing interviews and speaking in front of large groups—things she never would have imagined doing just a few years prior.

Lana learned that the project process makes you take a step back and understand your own strengths and weaknesses. She used to be someone who tried to do everything on her own, relying solely on her skill set. But the project taught her the value of teamwork and the importance of not being afraid to ask for help. She realized that if you have a goal in mind and the drive, you can accomplish anything in this world. She often thought of her favorite quote: "You're braver than you believe, stronger than you seem, and smarter than you think" (Christopher Robin in A.A. Milne's *Winnie the Pooh)*. This mantra gave her the faith to push through the moments when her library sessions were empty, and the deadlines felt heavy.

Today, Lana is looking toward a future full of adventure. Her passion for helping others has led her to pursue a career as a doctor, a path she views as another great adventure in science. She wants to continue empowering others and helping them thrive, especially as a woman in STEM. She encourages every girl to find a cause she is passionate about, reminding them that no problem is too small to address. Lana's journey from a shy girl selling cookies to a global advocate for media literacy is proof that when you believe in your mission, you can inspire the world. She didn't just build a website or create a school group; she built a legacy of digital bravery that will protect students for generations to come.

Lakshanya's project is like the steady calibration of a digital compass: she realized that while the vast ocean of the internet offers endless horizons for exploration, it is also filled with hidden currents that can pull the unaware off course. By providing the tools for navigation and the courage to lead, she has ensured that her peers can sail through the digital age with their eyes wide open, turning every screen into a window of opportunity rather than a trap of the past.

Chapter 4
Passion for Planet

Haley Santos (Ep 107)

Roots In The Garden

Haley Santos grew up with the scent of damp earth and the bright colors of blooming flowers as her backdrop. Long before she began her project, her heart was already rooted in the natural world. She spent countless hours as a child wandering through the woods with her papa, discovering the forest's hidden wonders. These walks were more than just exercise; they were lessons in observation and appreciation for the life teeming beneath every leaf. Her grandmother was another major influence, maintaining her own backyard botanical garden. To Haley, that garden was the most magical place on earth, a sanctuary where she could get her hands dirty and help life grow. "I was super into nature as a kid", Haley recalled, thinking back to how she loved taking dirt and planting flowers in her own little patch of the backyard. These early memories laid the foundation for environmental stewardship that would eventually blossom into her project focus. She remembered the way the sunlight filtered through the trees and the quiet dignity of the plants her grandmother tended so carefully. It wasn't just about beauty for Haley; it was about the connection between humans and the earth that sustains them.

As she entered high school, Haley's interest in nature evolved into a desire for advocacy. She joined a group called Youth Leadership NASA, where her team was tasked with tackling a social issue. Her group chose environmentalism and began a beautification project at a local high school. While this was a great start, Haley realized that she wanted to take the initiative even further. She saw that while many people enjoyed nature, very few understood the small, daily actions they could take to protect it. She decided to use her background as a Girl Scout to launch her own environmental organization called Gaia's Passion. This project wouldn't just be about one event; it would be a monthly commitment to educating her community about sustainability, biodiversity, and conservation. She wanted to bridge the gap between enjoying nature and actively preserving it. She knew that her community in the Gateway Council area had the heart for change but needed a leader to provide the resources. By partnering her organization with the NASA leadership group, she created a powerful springboard for her project. She began to see herself not just as a student who loved gardens, but as a change-maker who could organize events, lead workshops, and inspire her peers to see the environment through a new lens.

Building The Educational Forest

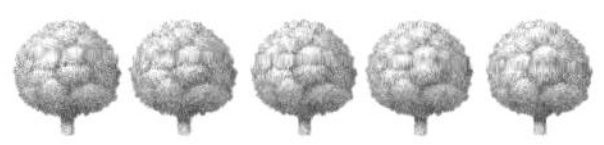

Once the vision for her project, Gaia's Passion, was clear, Haley had to figure out how to make her message stick amid distractions. She realized that to be taken seriously as a young leader, she needed a professional presence. She didn't want to post random pictures; she wanted to create an educational hub, which required her to master digital marketing and graphic design. Haley had a long history with art, and she decided to use those skills to give her project a distinct and beautiful brand. She spent hours on the computer, ensuring that every flyer and social media post was as vibrant as the nature she was trying to save. She found that Canva was her best friend when it came to leading a project. Whenever she felt stuck or wasn't sure how to present a new topic, she would scroll through the platform for inspiration. This effort to connect with her community through engaging content helped her see her role in environmental activism as meaningful and within reach.

To carry out her project with high quality and ensure people learned something, Haley had to be incredibly organized. She planned a different theme for each month, ranging from shopping sustainably to conserving water at home. She even took her organization to the local community market to engage with people face-to-face. To keep the project professional and sustainable, she focused on several key operational steps:

> **Designing** all her organization's logos, flyers, and educational presentations using digital

tools to ensure a high-quality and consistent brand image.

Establishing business accounts on Facebook and Instagram so she could track data on how many people were viewing and sharing her informational posts.

Partnering with the Callahan Community Market to secure a booth where she could advertise her organization and give away reusable products.

Authoring a coloring and activity book for children to reach a younger audience.

Haley found that her extensive social media presence enabled her to measure her impact in real time. By looking at her statistics, she could see which topics resonated most with her followers and adjust her strategy accordingly. This data-driven approach turned her passion project into a legitimate organization. She wasn't just a girl with a garden anymore; she was a social media manager and environmental educator reaching hundreds of people through their screens and in their neighborhoods. She even started a series highlighting Hispanic environmentalists during Hispanic Heritage Month, ensuring her project reflected the community she served.

The Hurdles Of The Courtyard

Despite her digital success, Haley faced significant challenges in bringing her project to life in the physical world. Her first big event was a school beautification project where she planned to plant native species in a courtyard. She thought that working with her high school friends would be easy because they were all in leadership roles together. However, she quickly learned a difficult lesson about team management. Because her friends were involved in so many other clubs and sports, it was nearly impossible to get everyone on the same schedule. She had to learn to be persistent and flexible, sometimes practically dragging people to the events to get the work done. This experience taught her that leadership isn't just about having a great idea; it's about moving a group toward a common goal.

Another major roadblock appeared when she had to change her project advisor mid-way through the mission. Her first advisor, Tracey Branson, was the head of the environmental science department and an amazing resource, but she became too busy to maintain contact. During the summer months, Haley found it nearly impossible to reach her via school email, which could have derailed the entire project, but she didn't give up. She pivoted and reached out to Meredith Cohen, a social worker she had known since the sixth grade. This switch was a turning point. Because they already had a strong personal connection, communication became much smoother, and the second half of the project moved forward at a much faster pace.

Haley realized that finding the right support system is just as important as the work itself.

Haley also had a moment of pure panic near the end of her project. While reviewing the requirements for the final presentation, she realized she had completely overlooked the global impact section. It was a holiday weekend, and her council was on break, leaving her to wait in suspense. She sent frantic emails, worried that her years of work might not count. When they finally replied, they told her she could have used her social media for that requirement, but by then, Haley had already taken it a step further. She decided to create a coloring and activity book for kids to ensure her message reached a younger audience. This challenge pushed her to create one of the most lasting pieces of her project, proving that a setback can often lead to a greater accomplishment if you stay persistent.

Microplastic Wake-Up Call

As Haley's research deepened, she encountered facts that changed her own lifestyle. One of the most shocking things she learned was that because of the massive amount of microplastics in the ocean, the average person consumes enough plastic to equal an entire credit card every month or so. This fact was so disturbing to Haley that it inspired an essay for her literature class and became a central talking point in her presentations.

She realized that environmentalism wasn't just about pretty flowers and clean courtyards; it was about the very health of humanity. This new knowledge added a sense of urgency to her monthly workshops. She wasn't just sharing hobbies; she was sharing survival skills for a changing world.

The community feedback was overwhelmingly positive, even if getting people to the events remained a struggle. Every time someone attended a workshop, they left with a five-star review of their experience. Haley loved seeing the super-positive reviews on her Facebook page, as they validated all the time she spent researching and planning. Her favorite memory was the first school beautification event. It was the moment when everything became tangible. She met students from her school, some of whom she had never spoken to before, who came out to support her mission. They planted six native plants in the courtyard, and Haley still feels a sense of pride when she walks past and sees them alive and thriving today.

Through her surveys, Haley found that people were learning from her work. They were learning how to compost and how to shop for reusable products. The measurability of her project wasn't just in the number of plants or the likes on a post; it was in the shift in mindset she saw in her peers. She had successfully moved the needle from a general "nature is nice" attitude to a specific "I can make a difference" mentality. By sharing her passion, she had empowered others to join her in the fight for a cleaner, healthier planet. She realized that her voice had weight and that her actions were creating ripples of awareness that reached far beyond the high school courtyard.

Passing The Torch

As Haley approached the end of her high school career, she had to think about the future of Gaia's Passion. A key part of a successful project is ensuring it lives on after the creator moves on. Haley decided to pass her organization down to a younger girl in her troop, Samantha Walman. Transitioning from being the sole leader to becoming a mentor was a moment of growth for Haley. She wanted to ensure that Samantha had the same opportunities to grow and lead that she had experienced. This transition ensured that the monthly workshops and community presentations would continue to serve the town long after Haley left for college.

The skills Haley built during her project have directly influenced her career path. She discovered a love for the logistical side of leadership— organizing people, managing schedules, and ensuring a vision comes to life —which led her to choose a major in stage management with a minor in marketing at Montvallo University. She realized that running an environmental organization is very similar to running a theatrical production; both require communication, problem-solving, and a lot of heart. Her project gave her the confidence to step out of her shell, conduct interviews, speak with administrators, and lead a team of peers. She graduated from high school with an associate's degree already in hand, ready to take on the world.

Haley's journey from a shy child walking in the woods to a national scholarship recipient is a testament to what happens when you follow your heart. She credits her success to her strong support system, including her parents, her troop sisters Bonnie and Sam, and her dedicated leaders. She encourages every girl to find a topic they are truly passionate about, because that passion is the fuel that will keep them going when the hours get long and the deadlines get stressful. Haley Santos didn't just earn an award; she grew into a leader who understands that while we only have one earth, we also have the power to save it, one plant and one person at a time. She proved that even a small troop of ten can change the world if they stay close and support one another until the end.

Haley's project is like a carefully tended garden: it began as a small, personal seed of interest planted in the fertile soil of her childhood memories, and through the unpredictable seasons of high school and the storms of rejection, she nurtured it with the sunlight of her passion. Today, that garden has grown into a sturdy thicket of community awareness, proving that when one girl chooses to cultivate change, she creates a landscape of hope where future generations can truly flourish.

37

Chapter 5
Different Brain Architect

Piya Scielzo (Ep 148)

Hidden Geography Of Thinking

For Piya Scielzo, the journey toward becoming a national advocate began in a very quiet place. Growing up, she attended a small school where the days were predictable, but her experience of them was not. Piya knew that her brain worked differently from many of her classmates. She saw the world through a lens of neurodiversity, a term referring to the normal variations in the human brain that can present as autism, ADHD, Tourette's syndrome, or a variety of other unique ways of processing information. However, in that small environment, her challenges weren't recognized.

"Growing up neurodiverse, I went to a really small school, and I didn't really understand what the word neurodiversity even meant," Piya recalled. She spent years wondering whether her peers felt the same things she did, or whether they were navigating the same invisible hurdles during a math test or a loud assembly. Her teachers didn't use those words, and without a vocabulary to explain her experience, she felt underrepresented. It was as if she were trying to navigate a city using a map that didn't show any of the streets she was walking on.

When she transitioned to a larger high school, the world cracked open. She realized that she wasn't alone in her experiences. Others would benefit from accommodations that let them view a page of text as a paragraph rather than a puzzle. As a freshman, she took a bold step out of her shell and founded her school's very first neurodiversity affinity group. Meant to be a safe harbor—a place where youth could talk openly about their brains without fear of judgment. But as the group grew, Piya noticed something troubling. While the students were finally learning how to advocate for themselves, the adults in the building were still using that old, outdated map. She realized that for her community to change, she couldn't just teach the students; she had to educate the educators.

Safe Harbor For The Different

The meetings of the neurodiversity affinity group became the laboratory for Piya's project. Every week, she listened to her peers share their stories. They talked about the frustration of being misunderstood by a teacher who thought they weren't paying attention when they were just processing information differently. The common thread in all their stories was a communication gap. Teachers wanted to help, but they didn't always know how.

"A big piece of feedback I heard in my club was that teachers in our school didn't have the most updated education on neurodiversity," Piya explained. This feedback was the spark that turned a small school club into a massive mission. Piya realized that the current rules for teacher training were insufficient. In many places, teachers were only required to have neurodiversity training once every ten years. In the world of science and education, ten years is an eternity. New research is published every month, yet students were suffering because their teachers relied on information from a decade ago.

Piya decided her project would tackle this head-on. She didn't want to give just one presentation and walk away. She wanted to create a permanent shift in the culture of her school and, eventually, in her entire region. She envisioned a world where every student felt seen, and every teacher felt equipped. Her project wasn't just about handing out a list of facts; it was about building empathy. She wanted to show the school administration that neurodivergent youth have the tools they need to thrive in and out of the classroom when given the right environment. She was no longer just a girl in a club; she was becoming a leader ready to redesign how her school thought about the human mind.

Toolkit For Tomorrow

To turn her vision into a reality, Piya had to become both a researcher and a manager. She knew that to be taken seriously by the school administration, her work had to be high-quality and backed by experts. She reached out to her school's learning support team, the very advisors she had gone to when she had questions about her own classroom accommodations. They were thrilled to see a student taking the lead on such an important issue. Together, they dove into books and websites to find the most effective ways to explain complex brain functions to a room full of busy professionals.

Execution was the most labor-intensive part of the journey. Piya wasn't just making posters; she was creating a curriculum. She designed assemblies for her peers and professional development workshops for the staff. One of the most powerful elements she included was the student panel. She recruited five or six students to sit in front of their teachers and share their perspective on what it was like to be neurodivergent in their specific school. This direct honesty was a game-changer. Teachers were able to ask questions and hear answers directly from the people they were trying to serve.

Surrounding her work with a strong team allowed Piya to carry out the project with precision. To ensure others across the country could repeat the mission, she focused on several key actions:

- **Collaborating** with the school learning support team to ensure all educational materials were accurate and professional.

- **Developing** a comprehensive neurodiversity toolkit that includes a how-to guide for starting affinity groups in other communities.
- **Organizing** student-led panels to provide teachers with direct, real-life feedback on classroom experiences.
- **Distributing** her resources nationally so that youth in other states could have the same tools to help their own peers.

As the resources began to circulate, the project grew beyond the walls of her high school. She expanded her training to the entire DMV area—covering the District of Columbia, Maryland, and Virginia. She was no longer just helping her friends; she was creating a blueprint for a solution that could help thousands. Piya realized that her voice had weight. When she stood at the front of a room full of teachers and said, "Congratulations, you are learning how to support a new generation," she felt the rewarding power of leadership in action.

Breaking The Ten-Year Cycle

Even with a successful curriculum, Piya faced a daunting mountain of red tape. The biggest challenge was the administration's schedule. Getting onto the professional development calendar is notoriously difficult, especially for a student. She had to navigate multiple meetings with the head of diversity and the school principal to explain why her training was more urgent than the standard ten-year rule. "Ten years is a long time to go without updated training," she argued, pointing out that students were arriving in classrooms every year with needs that couldn't wait for a decade-old update.

There were moments of uncertainty in the beginning. Piya had to be insistent that her project deserved a place in the school's busy life. She learned that being a leader often means being the most persistent person in the room. Eventually, the administration agreed to host her workshops during the summer professional development sessions, a massive victory. Still, it also meant Piya had to dedicate her summer break to training staff. She didn't mind the sacrifice because she knew the impact would be visible as soon as the first bell rang in the fall.

The feedback was immediate and overwhelmingly positive. Teachers reported that the training gave them a new way to see their students. One student told her that having a resource like the affinity group changed their entire high school experience. Knowing that she could provide the very thing she had missed as a younger girl was the greatest reward. Piya realized that leadership wasn't about avoiding challenges, but about organizing yourself differently for the future. She had successfully moved the needle from a me-first mindset to a community-first mission, proving that a single girl's drive can change a school's policy.

Crown Of New Horizons

As Piya neared the end of her high school career, her leadership continued to bloom in unexpected directions. Because of the success of her project, she was invited to serve on the Girl Scouts of Nation's Capital Council (GSCNC) Girl Advisory Board. GSCNC is one of the largest councils, and Piya found herself working directly with the CEO and the head of diversity, equity, and inclusion. She used this platform to share her toolkit with thousands of other girls, parents, and troop leaders across three states. She was no longer just a student with an idea; she was an advisor for a national organization.

Her growth as a leader also led her to the Miss America organization, where she competed as Miss Montgomery County's Teen. She integrated her neurodiversity advocacy into her community service initiative, taking her message to the Miss Maryland stage and even receiving a proclamation from Governor Wes Moore. She saw the "crown as a crown of opportunities," a way to take her project to an even higher level of public awareness. The foundations she built through her Gold Award project—learning how to market an idea, give a business pitch, and speak with confidence—served her perfectly in the world of pageantry and public service.

Piya headed to college at UNCC at Chapel Hill to major in business and entrepreneurship. She credits her Girl Scout upbringing with giving her the entrepreneurial spark she needed to succeed. Her advice to any girl starting their own mission is to look back at their favorite patches or past projects and see where their passions lie. "Just go for your project," she urged. "You never know, you might do a project that could turn into something bigger than you've ever thought of." Piya's story is proof that when you believe in your mission, you can inspire the world, one unique brain at a time.

Piya's project is like a master architect designing a building with a universal entrance. While the world had originally built a narrow doorway that only a few could fit through, she used her voice to widen the threshold and add ramps of understanding. By creating her toolkit and training sessions, she ensured that the schoolhouse of the future would have enough room for every mind to enter and flourish, turning what was once a wall of silence into a permanent gateway of belonging.

Chapter 6
Bare Necessities of Kindness

Makayla Key (Ep 33)

The Silver Spark

Makayla Key knew that sometimes the smallest items could make the biggest difference in a student's day. Long before she began her Gold Award, she had already learned the power of providing basic needs through her Silver Award. During that earlier effort, she organized a sock drive targeting three local schools. She still vividly remembers the joy on people's faces when she delivered those donations. One memory that stayed close to her heart was walking into a school and seeing a social worker's eyes light up at the sight of the supplies. The social worker had asked, surprised, if the socks were really for them, and Makayla had been proud to say they were. That experience taught her that many families rely on counselors and social workers to provide specific items when life gets messy. She realized that if a student got mud on their socks or needed a fresh pair for the weekend, having a supply at the school could change their entire outlook.

As Makayla entered her final years of high school, she felt a pull to go even bigger and impact more of her community. She decided to take the core idea of her silver project and expand it into something monumental. This new mission would be called MAK's Bare Necessities. The name was a clever combination of the first three initials of her name and a tribute to the classic song from The Jungle

Book. She didn't want to just stop at socks this time; she decided to include underwear as well. She understood that these were the "bare necessities" that many people take for granted but are essential for a student's comfort and dignity. Her goal was to reach eight local schools, covering every level from elementary to high school.

Makayla's motivation was rooted in the belief that no student should have to worry about basic clothing while learning. She had seen firsthand how a simple donation could ease the stress of a peer's life. By choosing a project she was truly passionate about, she knew the hard work wouldn't feel like a chore. She had been in Girl Scouts since the fourth grade, and she was ready to use every leadership skill she had gained over the years to make this drive a success. She wanted to ensure that the social workers had everything they needed to support families in her local area. With a clear vision and a heart for service, Makayla began the daunting task of organizing a community-wide movement.

Eight Schools, Eight Stories

Managing a project involving eight schools was like trying to direct a massive orchestra with performers in different rooms. Makayla quickly discovered that every school had its own rhythm and its own way of doing things. Some schools responded to her emails quickly, while others required constant follow-up and patience. She found herself playing phone tag with principals and administrators as she tried to coordinate the logistics of the drive. It was a major takeaway for her to learn how to interact with so many different professional personalities. She had to remain professional and steady even when communication grew rocky or when she missed a return call.

One unique challenge of the project was that some social workers served students in multiple locations. Makayla had to coordinate with a social worker who managed two schools simultaneously, requiring her to be twice as organized to ensure that neither school was overlooked. She realized that the project's success depended on her ability to keep all these moving parts functioning properly. She wasn't just a student anymore; she was a project manager overseeing a network of community leaders. She had to ensure everyone involved was fully informed and every question answered so the donation deliveries could go off without a hitch.

The organization of the drive was the biggest test of Makayla's leadership. She had to manage her team members' schedules from the National Honor Society, ensuring they were ready for packaging and delivery days. She also had to make sure they were dressed appropriately and arrived on time when visiting the schools. There were moments when things felt a little shaky, but she learned to figure it out as she went. She understood that perfection wasn't always possible, but persistence was. This phase of the project taught her that being a leader means being the person who holds the map when the road gets confusing. By keeping her ducks in a row, she ensured that the mission of MAK's Bare Necessities stayed on track despite the communication woes.

NHS Army and the Sorting Room

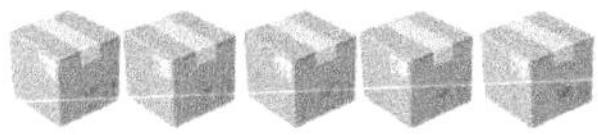

To collect enough items for eight schools, Makayla knew she needed a massive outreach strategy. She and her team didn't just rely on one method; they used every tool available to them. They held donation drives, reached out to supporters on Instagram and Facebook, and even set up an Amazon wish list to make giving as easy as possible. The community response was overwhelming. Makayla worked closely with several school organizations to power the collection process. Her team of volunteers was an impressive group that helped her manage the thousands of items that began to pour in.

To keep the project organized and ensure the community remained engaged, Makayla and her team followed a very specific execution cycle:

- **Publicize** the mission at least ten times across social media and in-person meetings to ensure the community hears the call for help.
- **Collaborate** with the National Honor Society and the PTSA to recruit volunteers for the heavy lifting of sorting and packaging.
- **Coordinate** with school social workers via email and the GroupMe application to set precise delivery times before the holiday breaks.

The influx of donations was so large that Makayla had to adjust her delivery schedule. Initially, she had planned to deliver everything before the Christmas break, but the community's generosity allowed for a first wave of deliveries before Thanksgiving. Sorting through 520 pairs of socks and 250 pairs of underwear was a grueling task that required hours of dedication. Makayla used the National Honor Society's monthly meetings to provide updates and keep her team motivated. She used email and messaging apps to keep her peers on the same page, ensuring consistency in every box's content and labeling them correctly for the right school.

Through this process, Makayla discovered the importance of clear communication. She learned that whether she was talking to a student volunteer or a school principal, her message needed to be consistent. She even sent out surveys at the end of the project to find out what people liked and how she could improve the drive for the following year. The survey results were positive across the board, which gave her the confidence that she had done a great job. She realized that she wasn't just collecting clothes; she was building a system of support that the community could rely on. The success of the sock-and-underwear army proved that when a girl takes charge, the community is more than willing to follow her lead.

Lessons and Laughter

One of the most rewarding parts of Makayla's project was a component she hadn't even thought of when she first started. As the deliveries were finishing up, she realized she still wanted to do more for the students before the Christmas break. She decided to visit three different schools to interact with the kids on a more personal level. At the elementary schools, she and her team sat down to read to the children. They chose interactive books like *No David!* and *Don't Let the Pigeon Drive the Bus!* Hearing the little kids shout "No, David!" and laugh along with the stories was a highlight of the entire journey for Makayla. They even brought coloring pages of socks and stockings to make the visit festive and fun.

At the middle school level, Makayla transitioned from a reader to a mentor. She organized a panel discussion for eighth-graders about what they should expect when they move up to high school. The younger students had many questions about the teachers and the workload, and Makayla was happy to offer honest advice. She remembered what it felt like to be in their shoes, and she wanted to make the transition a little less scary for them. This interaction allowed her to see the impact of her project beyond just the physical donations. She was providing the students with the "bare necessities" of knowledge and confidence for their future.

The social workers' gratitude was another powerful reminder of the project's success. Many appreciated that Makayla chose their schools without asking for help. "We picked you," she would tell them as she handed over the boxes of socks and underwear. Knowing that she had reached 52,000 lives globally through her cumulative efforts was almost too big to process, but the smiles of the individual kids in the classrooms made it real. Makayla had successfully started the conversation about student needs and had left a legacy that would continue through future annual drives. She had proved that being a leader means looking for the gaps in your community and being the one brave enough to fill them.

Scholar of Life

The growth Makayla experienced during her project helped her prepare for a future that was already looking incredibly bright. Her project work had taught her to handle international-level logistics and manage complex teams. This confidence served her well when she applied for the Jack Kent Cook Young Scholars program. As a Young Scholar, she had the opportunity to travel to different universities across the country during her summer breaks to explore her talents. She studied psychology at Lafayette College, black history at Northwestern University, and civic leadership at the University of California at Berkeley. She even spent a summer studying sociology with a professor from the University of Connecticut.

These summer programs were immensely shaping for Makayla, helping her develop a broader perspective on the world. At Berkeley, she focused on service learning and researched the causes of California's large homeless population. She wanted to understand how she could help solve these complex social issues, just as she had tackled the clothing needs in her own community. These experiences built her personal repertoire and made her a stand-out candidate for college. By the time she reached her senior year, she had been accepted into the University of North Carolina at Chapel Hill as both a Morehead-Cain Scholar and a Jack Kent Cook College Scholar.

Makayla's advice to other girls is never to give up, even when things get difficult. She knows that the journey can be frustrating and even defeating at times, but she believes the impact you make on others is always worth the struggle. "While you are doing this project to earn an award, it is bigger than just yourself," she reminds those who are just starting. Her journey from a middle school sock drive to a nationally recognized scholar proves that one girl can change the world. Makayla Key's story is a reminder that the bare necessities of life are not just clothes and food, but the courage and kindness we share.

Makayla's project was like a single stitch that eventually helped mend the fabric of her entire community. She realized that basic needs are a foundation for every student's success, and she dedicated herself to ensuring that foundation was solid. Makayla adapted her vision to fit the needs of eight different schools, proving that a leader doesn't need to follow a perfect recipe to create something special. Her legacy of "bare necessities" will continue to provide warmth and comfort to students for years to come, a reminder that one girl's decision to give back can create a ripple of kindness that never ends.

Chapter 7
Shield Against the Needle

Poppy Swallow (Ep 76)

Poppy Swallow, a Howard High junior, created vaccine distraction kits for children ages 5-11 now eligible for a COVID-19 vaccine. Swallow deliverd the kits to the Howard County Health Department at their new vaccine clinic location at Duncan Hall on the campus of Howard Community College on Thursday, Nov. 4, 2021. (Brian Krista/Baltimore Sun Media)

Shift in the Winds

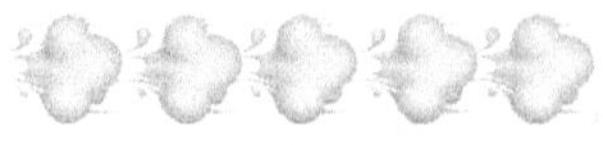

Poppy Swallow was a high school freshman when she first began dreaming of a way to change her community. Like many students her age, she knew that the world could be a scary place, especially for children who didn't understand the complex science of health and medicine. For Poppy, the fear of a doctor's office wasn't just a distant memory; she could still recall the sharp, clinical smell of the waiting room and the rising anxiety that came with the mention of the word shot. She realized that for many young kids, the fear of a needle was a massive barrier that made a simple medical appointment feel like a mountain to climb. She wanted to build a bridge over that fear.

Her original vision was local. She planned to design and distribute distraction kits for children visiting general pediatric centers. She wanted to fill these kits with toys and information that would make a routine check-up feel less like an ordeal and more like a moment of empowerment. But as she began to outline her project in the early months of 2020, the world suddenly shifted. The COVID-19 pandemic arrived like a sudden gust of wind, shutting down schools, businesses, and the very medical offices Poppy had intended to visit. For a while, the initiative she was so passionate about had to be put on hold as the world entered quarantine.

Instead of letting the pandemic deflate her spirit, Poppy used the time to reflect on how her mission could evolve. She watched the news and saw that a global effort was underway to develop vaccines that could bring the world back to normal. She realized that once these vaccines were available, millions of children would be heading to clinics— not just their regular doctors' offices, but massive, crowded vaccination sites that could be even more intimidating than a local clinic. She saw that her project wasn't just relevant; it was more meaningful than ever. She decided to pivot her focus, choosing to target the specific needs of children receiving the COVID-19 vaccine.

By shifting her focus from general pediatrics to mass vaccination sites, Poppy was stepping into the middle of a historic global event. She knew that her community needed a leader who could see public health through a child's eyes. She wanted to ensure that the memory of getting a vaccine was marked not by fear, but by the comfort of a helping hand and a well-timed distraction. With this new, refined goal, Poppy was ready to launch her project into a world that was desperately waiting for a little bit of sunshine.

Toolbelt of Kindness

Turning a grand idea into a physical reality required Poppy to become a researcher, a designer, and a project manager all at once. She knew that to distract a child, the items in her kits had to be engaging and tactile. She spent hours researching different types of fidget toys, looking for those small enough to fit in a portable bag but interesting enough to capture a child's imagination. She didn't just want random trinkets; she wanted tools that would engage the senses and ground a child in the present moment, rather than letting their mind wander toward the impending needle.

Poppy's team was small but dedicated. Because she was still under sixteen for much of the project, she didn't have a driver's license, so her mother served as her personal chauffeur, driving her to clinics and supply stores across the county. Her aunt, who worked at the prestigious Johns Hopkins Hospital, provided professional insight into medical environments and helped Poppy understand the logistics of clinic operations. Together, they turned Poppy's home into a hub of activity, assembling hundreds of kits and printing brochures. Poppy was the architect of every step, ensuring that her vision for these kids stayed on track.

The execution of the project was a lesson in meticulous planning and professional outreach. To ensure the mission reached the right hands and had a lasting impact, Poppy followed a very specific development cycle:

- **Sourcing** hundreds of fidget toys and distraction items that met safety standards for young children.

- **Designing** easy-to-read informational brochures that explained the importance of vaccines to both parents and their kids.
- **Coordinating** with the Howard County Health Department to place resources in their facilities for long-term use.
- **Assembling** over 300 individual distraction kits that were ready for immediate distribution at mass vaccination sites.

Beyond the physical kits, Poppy knew that her project needed a brain—a way to educate the community on why vaccines were so important in the first place. She spent significant time writing and refining the brochures, making sure the language was accessible and not intimidating. She even had the opportunity to tour the Howard County Health Department, where she saw firsthand how vaccines are stored and how clinics are organized. This tour gave her a deeper appreciation for the quiet heroes of the medical field. By the time her first batch of 300 kits was ready for delivery, Poppy had built more than just a collection of toys; she had engineered a support system that would help hundreds of families navigate a difficult time with a little more grace and a lot less fear.

Knocking on Doors

One of the biggest hurdles Poppy faced was one many girls encounter when taking on high-level projects: the challenge of being taken seriously by busy adults in professional fields. Because she was working in the middle of a pandemic, medical professionals were often overworked and difficult to reach. Poppy found that many clinic websites didn't list a direct phone number or email address for the site's administrators. She couldn't just send a message and wait for a reply; she had to find the courage to show up and speak for her vision in person.

She would often have to arrive at a vaccination clinic on the same day she hoped to deliver her kits and ask to speak with the site's head, which required a level of public speaking and self-confidence that Poppy hadn't always possessed. She admitted that public speaking was not always her strong suit, but she realized that if she didn't speak up for these children, no one else would. Standing before a clinic director, a high school student with a bag full of fidget toys, she had to clearly and professionally explain her research and the impact her kits could have. Every yes she received was a victory not just for her project, but for her own growth as a leader.

The logistical challenges were just as demanding. Because Poppy was a busy junior in high school, she had to balance her intense schoolwork with the constant assembly and distribution of her kits. She was also a dedicated athlete, and her schedule was often a puzzle of classes, practice, and community service. There were moments when the weight of the project felt heavy, especially amid the lingering pandemic stress. But Poppy was relentless. She knew that her deadline was her senior year, and she was determined to make every hour count.

Through this process, Poppy learned the value of persistence. She realized that being a leader meant rolling with the punches and being prepared for things to change at a moment's notice. She didn't let the lack of contact information or her own nerves stop her from reaching her goal. She discovered that most people are eager to help once they see a girl passionate about her cause. Her journey proved that even when the doors seem closed, a girl with enough determination can always find a way to knock loud enough to garner attention.

More Than Just a Toy

The true measure of Poppy's success didn't come from the numbers on her final report, but from a single, powerful moment in a clinic waiting room. While she was visiting one of the sites to deliver a fresh batch of kits, she witnessed exactly why her work mattered. A young boy was about to receive his vaccine, but the fear had become too much for him. In a moment of pure panic, he broke away from the nurse and tried to run out of the clinical area. The atmosphere in the room immediately grew tense as the staff tried to figure out how to calm the situation without worsening the child's fear.

One of the staff members who had been trained on Poppy's project quickly realized what to do. They reached for one of the distraction kits Poppy had provided and handed a fidget toy to the boy. The effect was almost immediate. The toy's tactile sensation and the sudden shift in focus allowed the child to ground himself. His attention moved away from the needle and toward the object in his hands. The moment Poppy had hoped for was happening right in front of her. The boy calmed down, returned to his chair, and received his vaccine safely.

That moment was a turning point for Poppy's confidence. She saw that her kit had shortened the time it took for that child to feel safe again. She had empowered that nurse with a tool that made their job easier, and she had given that little boy a memory of success rather than one of trauma. "It gave me confidence that my kits were being put to use," she reflected later. She realized she wasn't just a student offering a quirky, fun thing; she was an advocate actively making the community safer by helping the most vulnerable navigate a historic crisis.

The impact of her project continued to ripple outward as she distributed all 300 kits to various mass vaccination sites and smaller clinics. The

Howard County Health Department also displayed the brochures, which would continue to educate families for years to come. Poppy had successfully started the conversation about children's emotional needs in medical settings. Her project had transformed from a pile of toys in her living room into a county-wide initiative that stood as a testament to the power of a single girl's vision. She had proven that when we look out for the smallest members of our community, we make the entire world a little stronger.

Finding the Bullseye

As Poppy looks back on her journey, she can see how her time in Girl Scouts has shaped her into the confident young woman she is today. Her leadership growth didn't just happen during her Gold Award project; it was a steady process that began years earlier at Camp Ilchester. Starting in the eighth grade, Poppy had served as a counselor, teaching archery to younger girls. Standing on the range, she had learned how to give clear instructions and how to encourage others when they missed their mark. Teaching archery—a sport that requires focus, patience, and precision—was the perfect training ground for the public health advocacy she would later lead.

The discipline she learned on the archery range and through her project also translated into her life as an athlete. Poppy is a dedicated field hockey player, currently navigating the high-stakes world of college recruiting. She spends her weekends traveling to showcases, like a major one in Florida, where she plays in front of college coaches. She approaches her sport with the same organized mindset she applies to her kits, emailing coaches beforehand and keeping her ducks in a row to give herself the best chance of success. She knows that whether she is aiming for a goal on the field or a bullseye on the range, the key is to keep her eyes on the target and never give up.

Looking toward her future, Poppy's goals are as diverse and ambitious as her interests. She is torn between studying medicine, public health, or marine biology. Her project helped her realize that she has a deep passion for helping others through science, but her love for the environment and climate change research also pulls at her heart. She knows that whatever path she chooses, she will carry the skills she has gained—the communication, the persistence, and the ability to pivot—into her career. She encourages other girls to jump into their own missions, telling them that while a project may seem like a lot of work, it is a journey of self-discovery that is worth every hour.

Poppy Swallow's story is a reminder that when we aim for the heart of a problem with precision and kindness, we don't just hit the mark—we change the world for everyone watching from the sidelines. Poppy discovered that being a leader is often about finding the right tools to bridge the gaps in our community. Her kits were more than just fidget toys; they were armor that let children walk into a scary situation and come out feeling like heroes. Poppy crafted a mission that balanced scientific facts with emotional care. She is a reminder that the strongest bullseyes aren't from being quick like an arrow, but with the steady, patient aim of a girl who refuses to let fear have the final word.

Chapter 8
Power of a Young Voice

Amira Ismail (Ep 122)

Youngest Person in the Room

Amira Ismail was only 13 when she first stepped into the fast-paced world of political campaigns. While most kids her age were focusing on middle school dances or sports, Amira was navigating a landscape where almost everyone was at least twenty years older than her. She often found herself in rooms where conversations revolved around graduate school and long-term career goals, while she was still wondering what it would be like to enter the eighth grade. It was a very interesting and sometimes awkward situation. She vividly remembered being a fourteen-year-old volunteer, listening to coworkers discuss complex adult topics while she tried to find her own place in the conversation. She often didn't understand the vocabulary they used, and it was a struggle to navigate the weird emotions that came with being the only teenager in a sea of adults.

Despite her age, Amira was determined to make her voice heard. During the early days of the pandemic in 2020, she started helping with citywide efforts to get people to the polls. It was a strange time because many voters were nervous about waiting in long lines and didn't know how to vote safely. Amira realized the true power of her voice when family friends who had known her since kindergarten suddenly began looking at her differently. They realized that this young girl knew what she was talking about. This initial success gave her a spark of confidence, leading her to become a paid field organizer on the ground, talking to her neighbors about the issues they cared about most. She loved discovering why people thought the way they did and finding ways to help her community.

However, the journey wasn't always smooth. In 2021, a life-altering event occurred on a campaign, during which Amira felt she was treated unfairly because of her age and lack of experience. Instead of letting that experience discourage her, it pushed her to pave the way for other youth who wanted to enter the political world. She didn't want anyone else to feel the way she did. She wanted to create a space where young people could learn how to navigate the political landscape and be taken seriously, regardless of which political party they supported. She was ready to turn her personal struggles into a resource that would empower her entire generation to take a seat at the table.

Blueprint for Change

To turn her vision into a reality, Amira set out to create a unique three-day program called Make You Listen. She knew her peers were busy, so she chose a format that was impactful yet respectful of their time: one-hour Zoom sessions. She had to build the entire curriculum from scratch, which turned out to be the most time-consuming part of her project. She spent nearly 100 hours researching and writing, carefully pulling together puzzle pieces from various sources to create a cohesive, engaging experience for her participants.

Managing the requirements for her project was a major learning curve. She spent hours on the Gold Award website, often at 2 a.m. when she was bored, just playing around with the different steps to make sure she knew exactly what to do. Being the first girl in her troop to pursue such a high-level project meant she was figuring things out as she went, but she had great support from a staff member, Marlinda, who had also helped her with her silver project. Amira found that staying organized and disciplined was the only way to reach the finish line while balancing her schoolwork and other activities.

To ensure the program was a success, she focused on several key milestones during the execution phase:

- **Design** a comprehensive curriculum that covers civic engagement and political campaign strategies for young people.
- **Coordinate** with local experts and mentors to review the materials and ensure the information is accurate and inclusive.
- **Host** interactive Zoom sessions that let participants discuss their ideas in a safe, collaborative digital space.

Amira found that her friend Erin, who had created her own inspirational podcast, was a massive support system during this phase. Erin had gone through the process before and would constantly check in to make sure Amira was staying on track. Whenever Amira felt distracted, Erin would remind her that she had free time and should be working on her project. This kind of peer mentorship was invaluable. Amira realized that her team was more than adults; it included the strength of her friendships with other girls who believed in her mission. Together, they worked to ensure the curriculum was not just educational but truly impressionable for the youth who signed up.

Marketing a Movement

One of the biggest hurdles Amira faced was simply getting people to sign up. In a world where there is often a lot of mistrust, she had to figure out how to prove she was a real person with a real program. It was difficult to convince strangers to join a Zoom call at a specific time, especially as a teenager. She had to ask herself, "How do I get people to trust me?" She started by creating a dedicated Instagram account for her project. She chose the name Make U Listen, using the letter U instead of the full word, because she felt it would hold everyone accountable. Her goal was to make people realize that they should listen because youth voices were essential to the community.

Amira used a grant from her council to fund her marketing efforts. She discovered that Instagram had cool features that let her target her ads to other young people in her area. It was a proud moment for her when she attended a completely unrelated program, and someone told her they had seen her ad, which showed her marketing was working. Over time, as more people saw the flyers and the word spread through social media, the trust began to build. She realized that creating the first base of participants was the hardest part, but once the momentum started, the project took on a life of its own.

The program's impact was evident in how her participants engaged with the material. They weren't just showing up; they were taking a chance on her. Amira made sure the first session was incredibly great so that they would want to come back for the next two days. She found that her neighbors and peers were hungry for this kind of information. By the end of the three-day program, she had created a community of young people who felt more confident in their ability to advocate for themselves and their communities. She had successfully used her project to bridge the gap between young activists and the older political establishment, showing everyone that a girl's voice is a force to be reckoned with.

Taking the Lead at Council

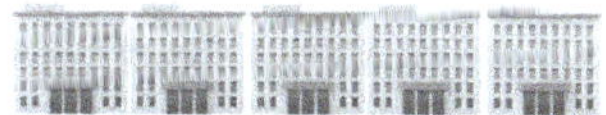

While she was working on her project, Amira was also deeply involved in leadership activities at the council level. She spent years participating in the Leadership Institute, attending Saturday seminars for weeks at a time. She explored different tracks, from learning how to code video games to diving into business and entrepreneurship. She even learned how Shark Tank works, questioning things like equity and business logic. But her true passion was always in the advocacy track, where she learned how to create campaigns and market herself. These experiences gave her the skills she needed to tackle a huge missing piece in her council: a girl advisory board.

Amira noticed that other councils across the country had advisory boards where girls could have a say in how things were run, but her own council in New York didn't. She felt this wasn't fair and decided to change it. In 2019, she approached the CEO, a woman named Meredith, and asked if she could pick her brain for a minute. Meredith loved the idea because she had participated in a similar board when she was a girl. Even though the pandemic pushed the schedule back, Amira remained persistent, pinging Meredith's email inbox every other day to keep the conversation moving. They met on Zoom for over a year, figuring out the bylaws and the governance structure needed to make the board a reality.

In November 2022, Amira faced her biggest leadership challenge yet: presenting the idea to the board of directors. It was her first board meeting, and she was incredibly nervous. She walked into a room filled with successful professionals and delivered a thirty-minute presentation on why the council needed a girl's voice. She told them that if they didn't approve the board, it would harm the girls in their community. Her courage paid off because the board approved the proposal unanimously. Afterward, many board members thanked her, admitting they should have had such a board sooner. Amira had proven that it only takes one girl's voice to change the entire governance of an organization.

Seat at the National Table

Amira's leadership journey eventually took her to the national convention, where she served as a delegate representing all five boroughs of New York City. It was her first time at a convention, and the scale of it was breathtaking. She was one of ten thousand Girl Scouts in a single hall, a sight she knew she would never forget. She had to learn parliamentary procedure and how to navigate the complex business of the national council session. She even joined a group chat on Instagram with 20 other delegates from across the country, where they shared memes and discussed the 7 proposals they would vote on over 3 days.

The experience was a true testament to the power of youth voices. Amira was surprised to see that the girls often spoke more than the adults during the debates. She herself was the very first delegate to stand up and debate a proposal on the first day. Her heart was pounding, and she was shaking with nerves, but she did it anyway. When she finished speaking, people from across the hall came up to congratulate her. She realized that even in a room full of more than a thousand people, a girl who isn't afraid to speak can make history. The convention wasn't just about business; it was about the sisterhood and the shared experience of being a leader. She bonded with other seniors in high school over the stress of college applications and the unique joy of being a Girl Scout.

As she looks toward her future, Amira is ready for the next part of her journey. She plans to study sociology in college and eventually earn a master's degree in public policy. Her dream is to work in lawmaking and legislation, ensuring that future laws don't belittle the diverse communities she loves so much in New York. She still finds time to be a junior counselor at camp, where her camp name is Uno because she claims to be the best at the card game. Whether she is leading a classroom of kindergarteners or debating on a national stage, Amira remains committed to the idea that you should never give up on what you're passionate about. She believes that if you trust your intuition and commit to your goals, you can overcome any obstacle that stands in your way. Her project was the spark that lit a fire of advocacy, and now that fire continues to guide other youth in finding their own voices. As she bridges into her future, she carries with her the knowledge that when a girl decides to make the world listen, there is absolutely nothing that can stop her.

Chapter 9
Digital Frontier Law

Chris McCarty (Ep 94)

Thirteen-Year Tapestry

For Chris McCarty, the story of leadership wasn't a sudden spark, but a slow-burning flame nurtured for over a decade. Imagine being part of the same small group of friends for 13 years, moving together from the simple days of being a 5-year-old to becoming young adults ready to influence the laws of the land. Chris belonged to a troop that stayed together through every stage of growing up, creating a bond that was more like a family than a club. This long history provided a foundation of trust and consistency, teaching Chris that major change doesn't happen overnight; it results from showing up year after year and deciding that the community's problems are worth solving.

Long before tackling the complexities of state legislation, Chris had already been practicing the art of the project. There were the early memories of the bronze and silver milestones, each one acting as a stepping stone toward a bigger vision. Those early efforts weren't just about earning a pin; they were about learning to identify a need in the world and realizing that a single person could do something about it. Whether it was a local service effort or a community awareness campaign, these experiences taught Chris the mechanics of making an impact—how to organize a team, set a timeline, and stay dedicated as the initial excitement faded.

By the time the final high school years arrived, Chris was looking for a mission that felt as big as the world itself. Having grown up in a troop that valued sustainable practices and long-term thinking, Chris wasn't satisfied with a project that would only last for a weekend. The goal was to create a legacy of safety and fairness that would protect people far beyond the borders of a single town. This personal motivation was rooted in a deep sense of justice and a desire to use the voice strengthened through years of service. Chris was no longer just a student following a curriculum; they were a pioneer looking at the digital world and realizing that the rules hadn't kept pace with the reality of the twenty-first century.

This thirteen-year journey had transformed a shy child into a confident advocate who knew the value of persistence. Chris understood that being a leader meant being the person who stays engaged when things get difficult. With a heart set on systemic change and a mind sharpened by years of community involvement, Chris prepared to launch a project that would bridge the gap between the playground and the state capitol, proving that the lessons learned in a small troop could serve as a blueprint for a more just society.

Mirror of the Screen

The inspiration for Chris's mission came from an unexpected place: the glowing screen of a smartphone. Like many people, Chris had noticed the rise of vlogs—online video journals where families share their daily lives with millions of strangers. At first, these videos seemed like harmless entertainment, a way for friends and family to stay connected. But as these channels went viral and turned into massive businesses, Chris noticed something troubling. While child actors on television or in movies had strict laws protecting their earnings and their privacy, the children appearing in these family vlogs often had no such protections. They worked, sometimes for hours a day, but the law didn't recognize them as employees.

This realization shifted Chris's perspective on the media we consume every day. Chris started reflecting on the specific criteria that differentiated a child appearing in a video from a child at the core of a program. On television, some regulations require a portion of a child's earnings to be saved for their future, but on social media, those lines are blurred and often non-existent. Chris saw a gap in understanding regarding the rights of these digital children. It was a silent epidemic of unregulated labor, and Chris felt a profound responsibility to bring this issue into the light.

The more Chris researched, the more they uncovered examples showing the problem was bigger than they first imagined. There were stories of children whose entire childhoods were documented without their consent, and who had no way to claim the money their parents had earned from those videos. Chris realized that this wasn't just a niche issue for a few famous families; it was a fundamental question of privacy and fairness in the digital age. "I started noticing that the children are in middle school and high school right now," Chris noted, realizing that their own peers were the ones impacted. The project began to take shape as an effort to ensure that the stars of these vlogs received the same respect and legal protection as any other working professional.

The intent wasn't to be a critic of social media; it was to be an enabler of change. Chris didn't want to just complain about the problem; they wanted to find a solution built into the very fabric of the legal system. They knew that to make a real difference, they would have to step out of their comfort zone and into the world of policy and legislation. They had to learn how a bill becomes a law and how to speak the language of lawmakers. The screen had acted as a mirror, showing Chris a reflection of a world that needed a stronger set of rules, and they were determined to be the one to write them.

Drafting the Digital Bill

Turning a concern about vlogs into actual legislation was a journey into the deep end of the government process. Chris knew that a person with an idea could only go so far without a team of shareholders—people who had a stake in the issue and the power to help move it forward. This phase of the project required Chris to become a professional networker, reaching out to experts in child labor, privacy advocates, and even the lawmakers themselves. They had to prove that they weren't just a high schooler with a hobby, but a serious researcher who had done the work to understand the intricacies of the law.

The execution of the project involved an in-depth cycle of research and outreach. Chris spent hours comparing the different state legislatures, focusing on procedures in Oregon versus Washington. They discovered that each state had its own unique rhythm and regulations, and they had to adapt their approach to whom they were talking. Adapting wasn't a simple task; it involved cold emailing busy officials and preparing for meetings where they had to explain their vision in under a minute. They were learning that leadership is as much about organization as it is about passion.

To keep the project on track and ensure that legislative deadlines were met with professional precision, Chris followed a very specific action plan:

- **Identifying** and recruiting a diverse group of shareholders, including legal experts and child advocates, to provide feedback on the proposed protections.

- **Researching** the differences in legislative procedures between Oregon and Washington to determine the most effective way to introduce their ideas to state representatives.
- **Developing** a series of educational vlogs to explain the legislative process to other youth, using the very medium they were trying to regulate to spread their message.

As Chris moved through the halls of the state capitol, they realized they were starting a conversation about a topic many adults hadn't even considered. They learned how to find state-by-state regulations and how to interpret the dense language of existing labor laws. There were moments when the process felt like a swamp of paperwork and phone tag, but Chris stayed focused on their why. They knew that every meeting and every draft of the bill were steps toward a world where children's rights were respected in every corner of the internet.

By the time the project reached its peak, Chris was no longer just talking about change; they were actively creating it. They had learned how to manage international-level logistics—balancing their schoolwork with the demands of state-level advocacy. They proved that being a leader doesn't mean having all the answers from the start; it means being the person who is willing to ask the big questions and find the people who can help answer them. Chris's work in the legislature was a testament to the idea that a single person's vision can indeed influence the laws that govern millions.

Sustainable Advocate

Even as Chris navigated the high-stakes world of state politics, they remained deeply rooted in the values of sustainability that had been part of their troop for thirteen years. For Chris, sustainability wasn't just about recycling or planting trees; it was a way of looking at the world that prioritized long-term health and stability over short-term gains. This mindset influenced every part of their project. They weren't looking for a quick fix for the vlogging issue; they wanted to build a system of protection that would be enforceable for future generations of digital creators.

This focus on the future also applied to their personal growth. Chris realized that the skills they were gaining—the public speaking, the research, the ability to navigate complex bureaucracies— were tools they would use for the rest of their life. They were learning to be well-rounded person, balancing their interest In law with a passion for environmental stewardship. They saw that all these issues were connected; a society that respects the rights of its children is more likely to respect the health of its planet. This realization made their project feel even more urgent and meaningful.

However, advocacy wasn't without its personal challenges. Chris had to learn how to manage the what-ifs and the fear of rejection. When they emailed a major group or a state representative and didn't hear back, they had to find the resilience to follow up and try again. They learned that a no or silence wasn't the end of the road; it was just a detour that required a new strategy. "You miss 100% of the shots you don't take," Chris reminded themself, echoing the advice they would later give to others. They refused to let the complexity of the legislative process dampen their spirit.

Through this process, Chris discovered that their voice was a powerful amplifier of their generation's concerns. They served as a bridge between the youth who lived their lives online and the adults responsible for keeping them safe. Their commitment to sustainable practices and ethical leadership made them a standout advocate in the eyes of the shareholders they worked with. They proved that when a person stands up for what is right, they don't just change a law; they change the way their community thinks about its responsibility to the future.

Reviving the Vision

As Chris looks toward the horizon, their goals are as ambitious and diverse as their interests. Having completed their Gold Award and spent over a decade in Girl Scouts, they are ready for the next chapter of their journey. One possibility is a deep-seated desire to breathe new life into community health and support systems. Whether this means pursuing a career in medicine, social work, or continued legislative advocacy, Chris is determined to be a force for healing and growth in their community.

The project taught Chris that they can do amazing things, a realization that has given them the confidence to tackle any challenge that comes their way. They encourage others to jump into their own missions, telling them that the journey of self-discovery is worth every hour of work. "Don't be scared of the grind," they advise younger students, reminding them that the lightbulb moments and the smiles of those they help are the true rewards of leadership. Chris has transformed from a follower of the troop's leader to a visionary ready to lead the world.

Their leadership continues to be shaped by their team's support and the memories of their 13 years in the troop. They remember the laughter around campfires and the feeling of achievement after finishing a tough badge. These experiences have taught them that true success is a team effort and that the most durable things we build are the relationships we nurture along the way. Chris knows that they will always be a Girl Scout carrying the values of courage, confidence, and character into every professional meeting and every community initiative.

Chris approaches life with a blend of scientific precision and creative joy. Chris McCarty's story is a reminder that while the digital frontier may be vast and unregulated, it only takes one person with a blueprint for justice to bring order to the chaos and light the path for everyone else to follow.

Chris discovered that leadership is like passing a bill: it requires a clear vision, extensive research, and the persistence to keep moving forward through every committee hearing and every no. Their project was more than just a legal proposal; it was a promise to the children of the future that their voices would be heard, and their rights would be protected, even in the fastest-moving corners of the internet. Chris worked with precision and heart to ensure that the laws of their community would provide a warm and solid foundation for the next generation, proving that when a person decides to lead, the impact can be as lasting as a statute carved in stone.

Chapter 10
Keeper of the Red River

Raina Applegate (Ep 164)

Tragedy on the Highway

The Red River National Wildlife Refuge in Louisiana is a place where the air usually hums with dragonflies and the rustle of wind through the marsh grass. But for Raina Applegate, a girl who spent much of her time volunteering there, the natural music was often interrupted by a much harsher sound: the roar of engines from the highway running right alongside the sanctuary. As she worked among the trees and waterways, she noticed a heartbreaking pattern. The very animals the refuge protects—turtles, deer, and squirrels—were often meeting a tragic end just a few feet from safety.

Raina had always been an animal lover, and seeing roadkill wasn't just a sad sight; it felt like a call to action. "I saw a lot of roadkill there because the refuge runs right next to a highway," she explained, recalling how even in her own neighborhood, she watched squirrels constantly darting into traffic. She realized that people weren't necessarily trying to hurt the animals; they simply didn't know when the wildlife was most active or how to share the road with them. The animals didn't have a voice to ask drivers to slow down, so Raina decided she would be that voice.

The motivation for her project grew from a deep desire to stop these preventable accidents. She didn't want just to be a witness to the problem; she wanted to create a solution that would change the way people behaved behind the wheel. She began to dream of a campaign that would educate the public and physically mark the danger zones. She knew that if she could get drivers to tap their brakes and keep their eyes peeled, she could save lives. This was more than just a volunteer task for her; it was a mission to bridge the gap between human progress and the natural world, ensuring that the Red River stayed a true haven for every creature that called it home.

Doodles with a Mission

Once Raina had identified the root cause of the roadkill problem, she moved into the planning phase of her project. She didn't want her educational materials to be boring or easily ignored. Since she loved to draw, she decided to use her own art to grab people's attention. She started by creating little doodles of the local wildlife, but she didn't just guess what they looked like. She carefully referenced actual photographs to ensure her drawings accurately represented the animals people might see on the road. This artistic touch became the heartbeat of her campaign.

Her plan was multi-layered, involving both physical signs and digital resources to reach as many people as possible. To bring this vision to life, she had to navigate several technical and creative steps. To carry out the project, Raina focused on these core actions:

- She drew animal illustrations on paper, scanned them, and colored them to create stickers and pamphlets.
- She partnered with two park rangers at the refuge to gather data on animal behaviors and the most dangerous crossing points.
- She designed and built large wooden signs for the refuge's entrance and exit to remind drivers to "Slow for Animals."
- She created a digital map to track the impact of her message as it spread through social media.

The creation of the pamphlets was a major part of her execution. She filled them with information on animal behavior, such as when they are most likely to be seen on the road and which times of year are most dangerous for certain species. By turning her digital drawings into stickers, she also found a way to fundraise for the more expensive parts of her project. She liked stickers and figured that if she enjoyed them, other people would too. It was a clever way to turn her hobby into a tool for conservation, proving that a girl's creativity can be a powerful engine for change.

The Price of a Sign

Even the best-laid plans encounter speed bumps, and Raina's project was no exception. One of her biggest challenges was a classic construction logistics issue. "I underestimated the cost of supplies for making the wooden signs," she admitted, noting she didn't realize how much the wood, paint, and hardware would cost. She couldn't just finish the entrance and exit signs and move on; she had to pause and figure out how to bridge the financial gap.

To overcome this, she had to dive back into fundraising with even more energy. She had to sell more stickers, which meant finding more buyers and managing the shipping process all over again. But the fundraising itself brought its own set of frustrations. In the world of online orders, things don't always go smoothly. Raina dealt with "people who would order stickers but then never give me their address or pay". It was a lesson in the realities of running a campaign—sometimes the hardest part isn't the work itself, but the follow-up and the administrative side of keeping things organized.

Another hurdle she faced was the waiting game of the approval process. She learned that when you are working with large organizations or council committees, you can't just send an email and forget about it. Her advice to other girls is to "check up with the council and not just wait for them to respond because they might not have gotten your proposal". Raina realized that being a leader meant being persistent and making sure others heard her voice through the noise of busy offices. By staying resilient amid the changes and unexpected costs, she ensured her signs eventually stood tall at the refuge, serving as permanent guardians for the animals.

Message Around the World

While the wooden signs protected the animals in Louisiana, Raina wanted her project to have an impact that stretched far beyond the Red River. She created a Facebook page to share her animal behavior pamphlets and roadkill prevention tips with a global audience. To track how far her message was traveling, she set up a map, asking people to mark where they were from when they encountered her project. The results were more than she ever expected. By the end of her project, she had reached people in 23 states and six different countries.

Seeing the notifications pop up on her phone was one of her favorite memories. "I had a whole bunch of people that would share it, and I would get like a bunch of notifications about it," she said with a smile. Her message had reached multiple continents, showing that wildlife conservation resonates with people everywhere. Inside the refuge building, she also installed a large poster board with information on how visitors could help prevent roadkill, ensuring that every person who walked through the doors left with a little more knowledge than they had when they arrived.

The measurable impact of her work wasn't just in the number of stickers sold or the states reached; it was in the conversations she sparked. People were suddenly thinking about the squirrels in their own neighborhoods and the deer on the highways differently. By using her art and her voice, Raina had turned a local problem into a worldwide discussion. She proved that you don't have to be an adult with a massive budget to have global links. All it takes is a girl with a plan, a digital map, and the courage to share her passion with the world.

Global Citizen

Raina's ability to think globally didn't happen by accident. She was used to transitioning and adapting, having been a part of five or six different troops over the years as her family moved. She even lived in Germany for a time, where she earned her silver award by creating a "Running Around Ramstein" patch to help other girls learn about German history and culture. Being a world traveler who had visited Switzerland and England gave her a unique perspective on how interconnected we all are. One of her favorite memories is a Harry Potter-themed patch program at the Pax Lodge in London, where she traveled by train to different filming locations.

These experiences as a traveler and a member of international troops shaped her into a confident leader. She learned to connect with new people quickly, noting that while every troop was different, they all shared the same spirit of service. Now, as she looks toward her future, Raina knows exactly where she wants to go. She is aiming for a career in conservation and climate change prevention. Her dream job is anything animal-related that lets her continue saving wildlife on a professional scale. She even hopes to visit every WAGGGS World Center in the future to collect the full set of pins.

Raina's journey from drawing doodles at her kitchen table to being interviewed about her international impact is a testament to the power of persistence. She wants other youth to know that if they have a big goal, they should not wait for things to happen. Just as her signs stand as a reminder to slow down, Raina's life is a reminder to keep moving forward, always looking for the next way to protect the world we share.

Raina's path is like the wooden signs she built—hand-painted with care and rooted deeply in the earth to guide others toward safety. Just as those signs stand at the entrance of the refuge to protect the silent creatures within, Raina's leadership serves as a beacon for environmental awareness. She learned that a single girl's art can travel across oceans and that a small doodle can represent a massive change in mindset. Her project wasn't just about preventing roadkill; it was about planting the seeds of conservation in every heart she reached, ensuring that the future of our planet is a little bit safer for everyone, one slow-down at a time.

Chapter 11
Courage to Stand Between

Christina Wiles (Ep 1)

Mirror Of The Past

For Christina, the journey toward leadership didn't begin with a grand speech or a massive billboard; it started in the quiet corners of her Vermont community, where she volunteered. Since she was five years old, Christina had been part of a Girl Scout troop dedicated to making the world better. She grew up moving from the simple joys of a kindergarten Daisy to the more complex responsibilities of a teenager. However, it was a single evening at a kids' night out event that changed her perspective forever. While she was helping provide babysitting for local parents so they could enjoy a night away, Christina noticed something troubling. A group of sixth graders was picking on younger students, using their size and age to intimidate those who were smaller.

The scene struck a chord deep inside her because it felt like looking into a mirror of her own history. Christina was honest enough to admit that she understood both sides of that dynamic. She had been picked on in the past, but she had also been the one being mean to others. After realizing how her actions affected people, she made a conscious effort to change her character. Seeing those middle schoolers repeat the same mistakes she had made settled in her heart. She didn't want to be a bystander who watched it happen; she wanted to create a support system that helped these students find a better way to interact.

She began to reflect on the nature of bullying in her local area. It wasn't just a school problem; it was a community problem that required a community solution. Christina realized that younger kids often look up to high schoolers more than they do to adults. If she could harness the "cool factor" of the older students, she might create a ripple effect of kindness. She knew her project had to be original and fit the specific needs of her town. She didn't want to follow a pre-written plan; she wanted to build a bridge from the ground up that would connect students across different generations.

Her personal motivation was to ensure that no other child felt the isolation of bullying. She understood that sometimes all it takes is one person to stand in the gap. Christina decided that her mission would be to create a mentoring program that fostered empathy and understanding. She was ready to take the lessons from her own life—the good, the bad, and the growth—and turn them into a blueprint for a safer school environment. With a heart set on advocacy and a mind full of ideas, she prepared to launch a project that would eventually be known as Arms Open.

Designing The Bridge

Turning a vision for a kinder community into a functional reality required Christina to dive deep into research and planning. She knew she couldn't just tell people to be nice; she needed a structured program that schools would trust. She started by looking at national models, such as the Big Brother Big Sister program. While she admired their work, she realized that using a national organization was often expensive and might not be feasible for her local community. Christina wanted to create something sustainable and free, something that belonged specifically to her town. She reached out to her high school guidance counselor, who eventually became her project advisor, to understand how a formal mentoring system functioned.

The planning phase was a masterclass in professional development. Christina and her counselor spent hours discussing the pros and cons of different mentoring styles. Initially, they considered connecting college students with high schoolers, but Christina kept going back to the image of those sixth graders at the babysitting event. She was determined to focus her efforts on the younger students who were just starting to navigate social pressures. Together, they decided to design a program that linked high school mentors with elementary and middle school classrooms, a significant undertaking that involved writing an entire program manual from scratch.

Christina treated the creation of the manual like a professional publishing job. She had to outline the program's specific goals, the mentors' responsibilities, and the activities they would lead with the younger kids. She didn't work in a vacuum; she held meetings with school principals to get their feedback and made several rounds of edits to ensure the manual met the schools' standards. She was learning that leadership is as much about the paperwork and editing as it is about the big ideas. She had to stay organized and patient, realizing that a solid foundation was necessary for her project to succeed.

The manual eventually became the backbone of the Arms Open project. It wasn't just a collection of papers; it was a published resource that provided a step-by-step guide for making the program work. Christina realized that her voice had power when she used it to structure a solution. She was no longer just a student; she was an architect of social change. By the time the manual was finished, she had a clear action plan and the confidence to pitch her program to the volunteers she would need to make it come to life. The bridge design was ready, and it was time to start building the physical structure.

Navigating The Red Tape

As soon as Christina began implementing her program, she encountered the reality of working within a school system: red tape. Her original vision was to have one high schooler mentor one specific younger student in a traditional one-on-one setting. However, she quickly discovered that this created major issues regarding liability and background checks. Schools have very strict rules about how adults and older students interact with younger children, which created challenges for implementing the project. It was a moment that could have discouraged her, but instead, it forced her to be flexible and think on her feet.

She worked closely with the school administration to find a workaround that would still allow the mentors to make an impact without violating any safety protocols. They decided to move the program into the actual school day. High school students would use their free blocks—periods where they didn't have a class—to travel to the elementary and middle schools for about an hour. Instead of being one-on-one, mentors would work with a group of students in a classroom setting under a teacher's supervision. This change enabled the program to help most students in a class rather than just a few individuals.

To get the program off the ground and ensure that she had enough volunteers, Christina had to become a master of publicity and organization. She followed a very specific execution cycle to ensure community engagement:

- **Publicizing** the project across multiple school platforms at least ten times to ensure that enough high schoolers saw the opportunity and understood how to apply.
- **Collaborating** with her guidance counselor to set up a training schedule for the new mentors, using the program manual she had written as the primary textbook.
- **Managing** the scheduling of all six initial mentors to ensure they could reach their assigned classrooms during their free blocks without interfering with their own studies.

Getting people to participate was one of her biggest obstacles. She learned that people are busy, and you must be relentless in sharing your message before they will act. Christina didn't just send one email; she posted flyers, made announcements, and talked to her friends until she had a solid team. She was learning the importance of persistence and publicity. By staying on top of logistics and being prepared for change at a moment's notice, she proved she could lead a complex operation through the most frustrating challenges. The project was finally in motion, and the "Arms Open" name was becoming a reality in the hallways.

Ripple Effect Of Kindness

The true measure of Christina's success came through the feedback she received once the mentors were in the classrooms. She didn't just walk away once the program started; she conducted regular surveys with both mentors and teachers to monitor progress. The results were more positive than she ever expected. Teachers began emailing Christina, reporting that they saw a noticeable change in the attitude and atmosphere of their classrooms. The younger students weren't just learning from the high schoolers; they were genuinely looking forward to their visits. Having a "cool" older student show up every week provided a level of engagement that adults sometimes struggled to achieve.

One of the most rewarding moments for Christina occurred when a mentor from her own troop approached her after a few weeks in the program. The mentor told her that she was enjoying the experience more than the students were, even though the kids were having a great time. She told Christina that she wished she had started doing this earlier and that it made her feel good to see the impact she was having on the younger girls. This interaction made Christina realize that her project wasn't just helping the elementary students; it was providing a meaningful leadership opportunity for her peers. The ripple effect was touching everyone involved.

The impact was measurable in how students interacted with each other. The bullying that

Christina had witnessed earlier began to decline as the younger kids learned new ways to communicate and build empathy. The "Arms Open" project was creating a culture where it was okay to be yourself and where older students acted as protectors rather than intimidators. Christina had successfully started the conversation about bullying and had built a sustainable system that schools wanted to continue. She had reached dozens of students in her local community, proving that a single girl with a plan could change the social fabric of her school.

Through this process, Christina discovered that she was capable of doing amazing things. The project had helped her build communication and interpersonal skills that she knew she would use for the rest of her life. She had learned how to manage a team, handle professional meetings, and stay dedicated to a goal through the ups and downs. Her confidence had grown significantly, and she no longer felt like the quiet volunteer she had been at the beginning. She was now a recognized leader who had made a lasting difference in the lives of hundreds of children.

Launching Into The Guard

As Christina looks toward her future, the lessons she learned through her project have prepared her for a path that is both unique and demanding. She has joined the Vermont National Guard, a decision that reflects her deep commitment to service and her community. While many people know that earning a Girl Scout Gold Award can lead to college scholarships, they don't always realize its impact on a military career. Because of the leadership skills she demonstrated through "Arms Open," Christina was allowed to advance two ranks upon entering the Guard. Instead of starting at the base level, she entered as a Private (E-3), which meant an immediate pay increase and a greater chance of earlier promotions.

This advancement was a direct result of her project work. It proved to the military that she could take on responsibility, manage complex tasks, and remain dedicated to a mission until the end. Even though she doesn't currently have a high level of responsibility in the Guard, she knows her background as a leader has positioned her to take on more significant roles soon. Her path is a reminder that the work a girl does in high school can significantly impact the opportunities available to her after graduation, whether she chooses college, the workforce, or military service.

Christina's journey has also included adventure and global exploration. She went on a two-week destination trip to Costa Rica, where she participated in the "Rainforest River and Reef" program. Not a vacation; it involved a treacherous ten-day, 30-mile hike through the rainforest. Christina had to zipline through the canopy and rappel down waterfalls, all while managing her fear of heights. These experiences taught her about emotional connection and personal reflection, lessons that she carried back to her project in Vermont. She learned that you must push yourself outside of your comfort zone to find out who you truly are.

Christina's story is a testament to the idea that when you lead with an open heart and a dedicated mind, you don't just finish a project—you build a foundation for a life of impact and honor. She is a reminder that the most powerful thing a girl can do is stand up and open her arms to those who need it most, proving that one person truly can hold a community together.

Chapter 12
Bridge To Belonging

Emma Fass (Ep 82)

Heart Of Peachtree Corners

🏛 🏛 🏛 🏛 🏛

Emma Fass grew up in a place where the scent of old paper and the quiet hum of community activity were as familiar as the air she breathed. The Peachtree Corners Library wasn't just a building filled with books; it was the center of her world. From her earliest days of father-daughter camping at Camp Misty Mountain, she understood the value of showing up for her neighbors. However, as she entered her teenage years and looked around her high school, she noticed something that concerned her. Many of her peers seemed disconnected from the world around them. While the adults were busy running the town, the teenagers seemed to be sitting on the sidelines, unsure of how to get involved or if their voices even mattered.

Emma decided to investigate the why behind this silence. She spent hours researching the issue and discovered a startling concept: a civic desert. This term describes an area where opportunities for people to participate in community or political life are scarce. Emma realized that even in places that weren't literal deserts, many teens were living in a state of civic drought because they lacked the education or motivation to take part in local life. She knew that if she could bridge this gap, she could help her generation find its place in the community. This personal motivation became the spark for her project, which she titled Caring for Our Community.

Emma was uniquely prepared for a challenge of this scale. Her life was already a masterclass in time management and dedication. She was a competitive athlete, spending nearly 12 hours every week in the pool with her USA swim club during the regular season. When she wasn't swimming, she was active in 4-H. She had even won public speaking competitions through 4-H, picking history as her favorite topic to present. These experiences gave her the discipline and confidence she needed to talk to government officials, coordinate with librarians, and lead her peers toward a future in which everyone played a part in making the community better.

The Blueprint For Connection

Planning the blueprint for connection required Emma to think like a diplomat and a project manager. She knew that to make her project successful, she couldn't just work alone. She needed to collaborate with the institutions that were already the heartbeat of Peachtree Corners. She turned once again to the library, seeing it as the perfect home for her mission. She didn't want a project that was just a one-time event; she wanted to create resources that would live on and continue to educate teens for years to come. Her vision was two-fold: a two-program in-person workshop series and a digital video campaign that could reach teens wherever they were.

To make this happen, Emma had to navigate the professional world of local government and library systems. Writing the proposal for her council taught her that a leader must be patient and prepared. The proposal (and the final report) might seem long and tedious, but she soon realized that the rigorous paperwork helped iron out the wrinkles in her plan and make her project more effective. Each question in her proposal forced her to think more deeply about her goals and flesh out her ideas. She also spent months developing a detailed program outline, which she then had to present to the Gwinnett County Public Library system for official approval.

Emma also realized the importance of building a strong team of advisors. She reached out to experts who could provide real-world insights for her project. She didn't just want to tell teens about local government; she wanted them to hear from the people who ran it. She coordinated interviews with high-ranking officials to give her peers a behind-the-scenes look at decision-making. By the time her planning phase was complete, she had built a support network that included government officials, librarians who helped with advertising, and the Teen Advisory Council at her library. She learned that being a leader meant being the person who brings all these different groups together to solve a shared problem.

A Weekend Of Action

With her team in place, Emma launched A Weekend of Civic Engagement, a Saturday and Sunday event held at the Peachtree Corners Library. Emma organized different stations where teens could learn about their neighbors' immediate needs and take part in activities that made a difference right away. Sunday shifted the focus to the environment, showing participants that caring for the earth is one of the most fundamental acts of a good citizen. The feedback from the attendees was immediate and heartening. They told Emma that the event made civic engagement feel fun and accessible rather than a chore.

Emma's digital component, the Civic Engagement for Teens YouTube series, was designed to expand her reach even further. The three videos she produced covered community service, environmental care, and the inner workings of local government. She wanted to ensure that even a teen who couldn't make It to the library could still find a starting point for their own journey. One of her favorite memories from the weekend was the environmental craft day on Sunday. She watched as the library room filled with laughter while teens turned recycled materials into art.

The project was carried out with a careful mix of creativity and organization. Emma wanted to prove that you could use your own unique talents to better the world. To ensure her mission was effective, she and her team followed a specific set of steps:

- **Interviewing** government leaders, including the mayor and a school board representative, to demystify the process of getting involved in local leadership.
- **Developing** hands-on activities, such as making wind chimes from recycled soda cans and bottle caps, to illustrate the importance of recycling in a creative way.
- **Distributing** educational materials and sharing the YouTube series link with other community groups to provide a permanent guide for future teen leaders.

The windchimes were a massive hit. Emma realized that when you give people a hands-on project that has a tangible result, the lessons behind it stick much better. By the end of the weekend, the participants didn't just walk away with a recycled craft; they walked away with the knowledge that they were part of something larger than themselves. Emma had successfully turned her research into a reality, and the civic desert she had feared was starting to look a lot more like a thriving community garden.

The Pandemic Pivot

However, the path to the finish line was anything but smooth. Emma's project journey took place during the height of the COVID-19 pandemic, which created a massive challenge for anyone trying to build community connections. When she first began the planning stage, in-person events seemed like a distant dream. Originally, she didn't even have an in-person component to her plan, which was a major disappointment because she truly believed that hands-on interaction was the best way to learn.

She leaned heavily on the digital side of her project. She faced intense personal growth. She had to manage her rigorous academic workload and her swim training while also becoming a video editor and a digital marketer for her YouTube series. Emma's patience was tested at every turn, especially when she had to make tweaks and edits to her project proposal to ensure it met high standards while remaining safe for the community. She learned that a leader is not someone who never faces obstacles, but someone who knows how to adapt when the original plan falls through.

The breakthrough finally came in August of 2021. The library began allowing in-person events again, and Emma moved quickly to add a hands-on component to her schedule. This transition from a purely virtual project into a hybrid success story was a masterclass in resilience. She proved that even in a world of social distancing, a girl with a plan could find a way to bring people together. By the time her final workshop ended, she had reached her goal of informing and motivating her peers, showing them that participating in town life didn't have to wait until they were adults.

Local Roots To Global Stages

Completing her project was just one of many ways Emma Fass demonstrated her commitment to being a global citizen. Even while her project was in its earliest stages, she became a United States youth ambassador to Ecuador through a State Department program. Emma learned about multiculturalism and community building with an Ecuadorian host family for six weeks. She even turned that experience into local action by hosting a Fourth of July food drive to address food insecurity in her own neighborhood.

Emma's life has been a tapestry of these international connections. She is always looking for the next way to bring people together, whether she is presenting a board on the country of Georgia for World Thinking Day or preparing for a destination trip to Italy to study cuisine and culture. During her Thinking Day presentation, she loved learning about Georgian Snickers, a traditional snack that looks nothing like the American candy bar. These moments of discovery have fueled her future goals. Emma plans to pursue a career in international affairs or languages, continuing her mission of building bridges across borders.

As she looks toward her college years and beyond, Emma carries the lessons from her civic action project. She has learned that the key to a successful mission is to know your topic well and be persistent through the administrative hurdles. She is a leader who knows that if you are patient and dedicated, you can turn the messy pieces of a community into something that makes perfect sense.

Emma's story reminds us that being an active citizen is like building a wind chime from discarded cans. It takes the quiet pieces of our daily lives—the books we read, the parks where we walk, and the people we pass on the street—and, with a little bit of creativity and heart, turns them into something that makes music when the wind blows. Emma didn't just build a project; she built a permanent bridge of belonging, ensuring that the next generation of teens in Peachtree Corners will never have to live in a civic desert again.

Chapter 13

Becoming a Civic Leader

Reflections Of A Visionary

As you conclude these stories, you have witnessed how personal history can turn into professional impact. You saw how a love for wildlife grew into hand-painted wooden signs that serve as permanent guardians of the marsh's silent creatures. You read about mentors who turned the pain of bullying into published manuals that build bridges between generations, proving that one person can hold a community together. These leaders didn't start with massive budgets; they started with doodles, scrap wood from a donor pile, and the courage to look at the bare necessities of their neighbors. They navigated civic deserts and the bright traps of the screen, proving that a teenager's voice is not a small thing—it is a slow-burning flame that can change state-level policies and influence the laws of the land.

The background of every project we explored was rooted in a deep sense of observation and justice. Whether it was creating distraction kits to shield children from fear during a global pandemic or establishing a Media Literacy Council to guard the digital gateway, each advocate faced the hassle of red tape and the silence of empty library sessions. They learned that leadership is as much about the paperwork and the thirty-second pitch as it is about the big idea. They moved the needle from witnessing a problem to engineering a solution, proving they could do amazing things. Their growth wasn't just in the awards they earned, but in the entrepreneurial spark that led them to national advisory boards and global stages. Now, their collective legacy serves as a blueprint for your own journey, reminding you that your voice has weight and your actions create ripples of awareness that reach far beyond your own backyard.

Bridging Into Your Mission

Transitioning from a reader to a leader means moving into the deep end of the implementation process and finding your own lightbulb moment. The stories you have read are not just inspirations; they are proof that the mechanics of making an impact—organizing a team, setting a timeline, and staying dedicated—are skills you can master. Before you dive into the toolkit provided in this chapter, take a moment to reflect on the mirror of the past. Like the advocates before you, your unique background—whether you are a world traveler, a competitive athlete, or someone navigating neurodiversity—is the foundation of your advocacy. You have seen that even a shy girl can transform into a confident representative of her community, literally carrying a banner of achievement through the streets.

Now, it is your turn to step out of your comfort zone and into the world of policy, engineering, or community service. This toolkit is designed to guide you through regulations and professional communication. You will learn to be insistent on your goals even when the initial response is cold or when you face the waiting game of the approval process. Leadership requires you to be the person who holds the map when the road gets confusing, managing schedules and navigating the red tape of school boards and council committees. By following these steps, you will move from identifying a gap in understanding to creating a permanent shift in your community's culture.

Prepare to be the enabler of change the world is waiting for.

Step One: Finding Your North Star

Becoming a civic leader begins with identifying a problem you are truly passionate about, as this passion is the fuel that will keep you going when the hours get long and the deadlines get stressful. Use your personal history as a mirror to find your mission. Whether you are an animal lover, a coder, or someone who cares about social justice, your background is your greatest asset. You don't have to wait for someone else to fix a problem—you can be the voice for the voiceless. To find your focus, you must become a keen observer of your environment, looking for civic deserts or taboos that others might have overlooked. Use the following guide to identify your spark:

- **Observe Your Community**: Look for gaps in services, safety, or inclusion. Ask yourself what is missing in your local schools or parks.
- **Research the "Why"**: Investigate whether a lack of education, outdated laws, or a civic drought causes a problem.
- **Identify Your Unique Angle**: How can your specific talents—like art, robotics, or public speaking—be used to solve the issue?

Don't be discouraged if your small idea feels overwhelming at first. Leadership is a slow-burning flame nurtured by showing up year after year. You must be ready to knock loud enough to garner attention, even when doors seem closed. Every major project, from protecting child vloggers to building a portable racetrack, started with a single person deciding that a problem was worth solving. Remember that "you miss 100% of the shots you don't take" (Wayne Gretzky), so find your bullseye and take that first step toward advocacy. Your growth as a leader starts the moment you move from being a witness to being the architect of a better world.

Step Two: Navigating The Action Plan

Once your mission is clear, you must move into the planning phase, which is a masterclass in professional development. Turning a vision into reality requires you to become a project manager who can handle the logistics of construction, the red tape of liability, and the drudgery of editing. You will need to build a team of shareholders and advisors—government officials, teachers, or experts—who can provide real-world insights. Your execution should follow a specific design loop to ensure high-quality impact. Use this blueprint to structure your project:

- **Draft a Structured Proposal:** Create a sustainable program manual or curriculum that meets rigorous standards.
- **Build a Professional Presence:** Use digital marketing and graphic design to give your mission a distinct and beautiful brand.

- **Master the Art of the Pitch**: Practice delivering a "thirty-second pitch" and writing clear, professional emails to busy administrators.
- **Be Persistent with Follow-Ups**: Don't just send one email; check in with your partners and team regularly.
- **Implement a Development Cycle**: Design, test, and improve your resources based on survey and student panel feedback.

As you navigate this stage, you may encounter speed bumps, such as underestimating the cost of supplies or dealing with unorganized volunteers. You must remain flexible and learn to pivot when original plans, like in-person workshops, fall through. Being a leader means being the most persistent person in the room, even when you are balancing intense schoolwork and sports with your mission. Your ability to stay professional and steady when communication becomes rocky will set you apart from those who don't finish.

Step Three: Sustainability And Global Impact

The final measure of a successful mission is ensuring it lives on after you move on and that its impact reaches as far as possible. You have seen how projects can span 23 states and six countries through global links and digital maps. A true leader ensures their work is sustainable by passing the torch to a younger mentor who can keep the flame alive. Ensuring your mission becomes a permanent shift in your community's culture rather than just a one-time event. Follow these steps to finalize your legacy:

- **Document and Measure Your Impact:** Use data, surveys, and global impact maps to prove the effectiveness of your work.
- **Share Your Resources Nationally:** Distribute your toolkits and digital brochures so youth or adults in other states can repeat your mission.
- **Create a Permanent Hub:** Build a dedicated website or group that serves as a lasting resource for future students.
- **Mentor Your Successor:** Identify a younger person in your troop or school to lead the project after you graduate.

By the time you finish your project, you will have built a foundation for a life of impact and honor. The skills you gained—public speaking, managing complex teams, and navigating bureaucracies—will serve you in college, the military, or any professional career you choose. You might find yourself debating on a national stage or advising the CEO of a major organization. Remember, the best things are often the ones you've worked the hardest to create. Your project was the spark that lit a fire of advocacy, and now that fire will guide you as you bridge into your future, ready to lead the world.

🩶 Make the world listen today 🩶

ABOUT THE AUTHOR

Sheryl M. Robinson is a podcaster, mentor, and speaker dedicated to helping teens and young adults discover their unique gifts, talents, and abilities, creating a path toward their dreams.

Sheryl holds a Master of Arts in Servant Leadership from Viterbo University and a Bachelor's in Accounting from Southern Illinois University – Carbondale. She has been a proud member of Girl Scouts for more than 30 years. Her passion for supporting teens — especially those pursuing the Girl Scout Gold Award — led her to create *Hearts of Gold*, a YouTube series and podcast featuring Gold Award Girl Scouts from across the world.

In recognition of her work elevating and supporting the Girl Scout Highest Awards, Sheryl has been honored with the GSUSA Thanks II Award, the organization's highest recognition for service.

Recognizing the need for younger Girl Scouts to have resources and role models as they pursue the Bronze Award and Silver Award, Sheryl created this middle-grade book series to share inspiring stories of leadership, courage, and community change.

She deeply believes that the Girl Scout Highest Awards not only make the world a better place but also transform the Girl Scouts who earn them — building lifelong changemakers, confident problem-solvers, and compassionate leaders.

ACKNOWLEDGMENTS

Creating this book has been a journey shaped by many remarkable people, and I am deeply grateful for each of you.

To **my mom, Jean**, who first started me in Girl Scouts many years ago and planted the seeds of everything that would follow.

To **my daughter, Nikki**, a Bronze, Silver, and Gold Award Girl Scout whose dedication inspires me every day. Watching you flourish through each phase of your life is one of my greatest joys.

To **my husband, Mark,** thank you for always supporting me and the many plates you quietly set beside me while I typed away. I thank God for bringing you into my life every day.

To **Rayna,** thank you for reading the first draft and sharing thoughtful feedback. Your insights helped shape this book and made it stronger.

To **all the Gold Award Girl Scouts** who have shared their stories on the Hearts of Gold podcast — thank you for trusting me with your journeys. Your courage, creativity, and leadership inspire thousands.

To the **Girl Scout leaders, volunteers, and parents** who support these incredible young women: your encouragement makes meaningful change possible.

To **Cassie**, who encouraged me to restart my Girl Scout journey when my daughter joined Girl Scouts.

A heartfelt thank you to **Stacie and Shannan**, who have listened to me talk about this book for years and never stopped encouraging me to make it happen.

To **Walter**, my podcast editor for the first nine years, and **Tommy**, my new editor — and to their entire family, especially **Greg**, whose podcasting challenge a decade ago helped set all of this into motion.

And finally, to **Elsie, Rob, Cliff, Daniel, and Jessica** — thank you for your inspiration, for keeping the process fun, for sharing your knowledge, and for helping Hearts of Gold continue to grow.

This project exists because of each of you.
Thank you for helping bring these stories to life.

To all the future Bronze, Silver, and Gold Award Girl Scouts and others inspired by this book – Be the change you want to see in the world and remember <u>your</u> leadership matters.

MORE STORIES

Want to hear more inspiring stories from Gold Award Girl Scouts?

HeartsofGoldPodcast.com

You can watch or listen to new episodes every month.

Podcast:
https://bit.ly/3JT7x0w

YouTube:
https://bit.ly/3P5nns8

Instagram:
https://bit.ly/3JZ2JX8